TEACHING STATE HISTORY

TEACHING STATE HISTORY

A GUIDE TO DEVELOPING A
MULTICULTURAL CURRICULUM

Ava L. McCall and Thelma Ristow

WITHDRAWN

HEINEMANN
Portsmouth, NH

Heinemann
A division of Reed Elsevier Inc.
361 Hanover Street
Portsmouth, NH 03801–3912
www.heinemann.com

Offices and agents throughout the world

Library of Congress Cataloging-in-Publication Data
McCall, Ava Louise.
    Teaching state history : a guide to developing a multicultural curriculum / by Ava L. McCall and Thelma Ristow.
        p.   cm.
    Includes bibliographical references.
    ISBN 0-325-00482-X
        1. United States—History, Local—Study and teaching.   2. U.S. states—History—Study and teaching.   3. Pluralism (Social sciences)—Study and teaching—United States.   4. Multicultural education—Curricula
    5. Multiculturalism—United States.   I. Ristow, Thelma.   II. Title.

E175.8 .M39   2003
372.89′044—dc21   2002038848

Editor: Danny Miller
Production editor: Sonja S. Chapman
Cover design: Night and Day Design, Suzanne Heiser
Compositor: Publishers' Design and Production Services, Inc.
Manufacturing: Steve Bernier

Printed in the United States of America on acid-free paper
07   06   05   04   03   VP   1   2   3   4   5

CONTENTS

ACKNOWLEDGMENTS

Our collaborative Wisconsin history project was made possible through support from both the University of Wisconsin Oshkosh and the Oshkosh Area School District. We especially thank the university's Faculty Development Program, Dr. Donald Mocker, former Dean of the College of Education and Human Services, and the Oshkosh Area School District for providing financial support for our project. We received funds to spend time in the summer developing Wisconsin history curriculum, to release Ava from some of her university teaching responsibilities in order to teach collaboratively with Thelma, to purchase trade books and other teaching resources, and to hire a research assistant. We are thankful to Kristen Bond Mueller, our research assistant, for her many contributions to the project. Kristen interviewed all the students, transcribed the interview tapes, videotaped lessons and activities, prepared instructional materials and bulletin boards, and helped students during many of our activities.

We are exceedingly grateful for the enthusiastic endorsement and encouragement to collaborate from Mrs. Patricia Vickman, Webster Stanley Elementary School Principal. Patti is dedicated to providing the best learning opportunities for children and rich professional development endeavors for teachers and staff at her school. She welcomes university and community involvement in Webster Stanley for the benefit of students. Mr. George Pouba, Deputy Superintendent, and Dr. Barbara Herzog, Assistant Superintendent for Instruction, Oshkosh Area School District, also strongly supported our project. We appreciate their generous financial contributions for teaching materials and encouragement to take risks for the sake of improving our teaching and promoting student learning.

We also extend our warm thanks to the fourth graders and their families who participated in our Wisconsin history project. Those twenty children have a special place in our hearts because they made teaching Wisconsin history exciting and rewarding. They responded with enthusiasm to our activities, learned from our curriculum, challenged us with their questions, and encouraged us to become better teachers.

Finally, we thank our partners, Bill Ristow and David Calabria, for their many avenues of support for us as teachers. They listen to our classroom stories and teaching ideas, assist in finding instructional resources, help us carry materials to school, and empathize with the many, many hours spent on our collaborative project. Bill and David understand that teaching is one of the most important, and demanding, professions and our commitment to "teaching to change the world."

INTRODUCTION

State history is a required component of the elementary social studies curriculum in all states. It is also challenging to teach because often teachers have at their disposal fewer resources than for such national topics as United States history or geographical regions of the United States. We invite you to participate in our journey to teach state history in ways that encourage students to see themselves and their families as part of their own state history, to learn about and appreciate their state's cultural diversity, and to take a few steps in the shoes of people who lived before them. We want students not only to understand, but also to empathize with diverse groups who influenced their state. At the same time, like all teachers, we need to address national and state social studies standards. School districts may require it and standardized tests may be aligned with these standards. Collaborating helped us accomplish our goals of balancing our commitment to teaching a multicultural state history with the requirement that we teach the standards. We drew on two educators' teaching experiences and expertise, knowledge of children, and curriculum resources. *Teaching State History* describes our collaboration as it unfolded in a fourth-grade classroom. The text describes our experiences with the hope that you can apply similar resources and teaching strategies to enrich your own teaching of state history.

TEACHING STATE HISTORY COLLABORATIVELY

Ava's View

When Thelma and I began our collaboration in the summer of 1997, I had taught elementary students for thirteen years in South Bend, Indiana, and social studies methods for elementary education majors for nine years, primarily at the University of Wisconsin Oshkosh. During my experiences in teacher education, I devoted a great deal of energy to developing a multicultural, social reconstructionist emphasis in my social studies methods course.[1] I wanted students to question traditional social studies content, consider different perspectives, and understand the connection between the people whose experiences were included in the curriculum and their power in society. I hoped my students would embrace a multicultural social studies curriculum as an avenue for creating a more equitable society. Some of them responded positively to this approach while some criticized it. Usually a few students each semester complained that my focus on including women of all cultural groups, Native Americans, African Americans, Hmong, and additional cultural groups in social studies was too strong. They questioned if teachers had time to create multicultural social studies curriculum, if school districts would allow teachers to make such curriculum changes, if other teachers and parents would criticize teachers who transformed the curriculum with multicultural ideas, and if elementary students could learn from such a challenging curriculum.

Collaborating with Thelma in developing and teaching multicultural state history curriculum was my opportunity to discover if I could "practice what I preach" in an elementary classroom. It would allow me to determine if fourth graders were able to learn from the multicultural ideas and teaching strategies I had been advocating for years at the university. I believed they would, but had no proof. Because the National Council for the Social Studies published the national social studies standards in 1994, a few years before our collaboration, and the state standards were not yet developed, I also wanted

2

to explore the compatibility between the national standards and multicultural ideas.

Thelma and I met in a graduate educational issues course I taught. She was completing her master's degree; throughout the course, I was impressed with Thelma's openness to diverse perspectives on educational issues. In addition, we both supervised prestudent teaching clinical students placed in Thelma's classroom. These experiences allowed me to observe Thelma's significant teaching skills, confidence, and willingness to take risks. Thelma also encouraged clinical students to use ideas, resources, and teaching strategies they learned in my social studies methods course with her elementary students. I was ecstatic when Thelma agreed to work with me in developing state history curriculum and teaching it collaboratively in her fourth-grade classroom!

Thelma's View

My career as an elementary teacher had begun thirty-six years before Ava and I began our collaborative project in the summer of 1997. Ava and I first met during the spring semester of 1994 when I was a student in her Issues in Elementary Education course as I was nearing the end of my master's degree preparation. During class discussions, different educational equity issues such as school funding, assessment, and tracking were brought to light of which, as a teacher, I had not been fully aware. Other ideas that were discussed confirmed my teaching ideas and practice. I appreciated Ava's honesty and her concern for total equality in education with no biases in race, gender, and culture. I had also worked closely with Ava as we both supervised clinical students who had been placed in my classroom. I became aware of new ideas and resources that Ava had introduced to the clinical students and these were proving very effective in my classroom.

I remember very well the day Ava called and asked if I would work with her on this project. My initial reaction was, "I don't need to get involved in any more projects at my age!" Once I realized that this project would involve collaborating with Ava, a university professor, to develop social studies units geared to studying our state and then work as a team in the classroom, I knew I had to find out more. After Ava commented that she wanted to spend time in an elementary classroom and test ideas she was giving her preservice teachers, I thought, "Aha! If someone is willing to come out of the ivory tower, I feel it is important to open my classroom for the opportunity. After all, do most university professors really know what an elementary classroom is like today?" My goal for the students in my classroom was to put them in a win-win situation. They would benefit from two teachers in the classroom, while at the same time, their classroom teacher (me) would be learning ways to be more effective in guiding them in their learning. Thus, I agreed to work collaboratively with Ava.

University and School District Support for Our Collaboration

We were fortunate to have the support from two educational institutions for our collaboration. We received financial support from Thelma's school district, and both the school principal and the deputy superintendent enthusiastically endorsed our project. We also received funding from the university's Faculty Development Program. The funding reimbursed us for the time we spent during the summer of 1997 developing a state history curriculum. It funded Ava's half-time release from university teaching responsibilities for the fall 1997 semester to allow us to teach together two and one-half days a week. It allowed us to hire a research assistant for the 1997-98 school year. Our research assistant, Kristen Bond Mueller, prepared instructional materials and bulletin boards, assisted students during some of our instructional activities, videotaped selected lessons, interviewed each student at the end of each unit about what they learned, and transcribed the interview tapes. We also obtained funds from the university and the school district to purchase instructional materials, primarily trade books, for our project.

MEET THE COMMUNITY, THE SCHOOL, AND THE STUDENTS

The setting for our collaborative state history project is the town of Oshkosh, Wisconsin, an upper Midwest community of approximately sixty thousand people with a strong German American influence and few people of color. Hmong immigrants began settling here during the 1980s and currently number approximately thirty-five hundred. The community traditionally has been conservative and slow to accept "outsiders" of any cultural group, and the Hmong in particular have not been well received. The influx of Hmong immigrants with limited English skills significantly influenced the local school district, necessitating the creation of English as a Second Language programs. Although the community has traditionally been and continues to be blue-collar, with the current greatest employment opportunities in manufacturing, there are also a growing number of occupations available in educational, health, and governmental services.

The K-5 elementary school in which we taught, one of the sixteen public elementary schools in the community, is one of the most diverse. At the time of our project, 53 percent of the students were considered below the poverty level (as defined by students' eligibility for free and reduced lunch) and 19 percent of the students possessed limited English proficiency (mostly Hmong). The school also served children living in sheltered care at the domestic abuse center.

Although the school's student population often fluctuated with children regularly leaving and entering during the school year, we were fortunate to have a very stable group of students during the five months of the project. At the beginning of the school year, nineteen students began the project with us and participated in the first two curriculum units. At the end of November, another student joined the class, leading to a total of twenty children engaging in the last two units. The fourth-grade students' backgrounds reflected some gender, cultural, and class diversity, including eleven girls and nine boys; six who qualified for free or reduced lunch; four Hmong (who were among the students entitled to free or reduced lunch); two Mexican Americans; one East Indian; and thirteen European Americans.

ENDNOTES

1. See Christine A. Sleeter and Carl A. Grant, *Making Choices for Multicultural Education: Five Approaches to Race, Class, and Gender,* 3rd ed. (Upper Saddle River, NJ: Merrill, 1999), 188–216.

CHAPTER 1

CREATING STATE HISTORY
CURRICULUM

Thelma works with a group of nine students in a literature circle to read *The Sacred Harvest: Ojibway Wild Rice Gathering.*[1] All children are participating in one of three literature circles, heterogeneously grouped based on their choice of text, literacy level, gender, and culture. The remaining two groups are also reading and discussing trade books, which portray Wisconsin Native people's food gathering and growing traditions. Thelma's group examines unprocessed wild rice and wild rice that is ready to cook. Although Hua is often quiet, she volunteers to demonstrate how to remove the outer husks from the unprocessed wild rice by winnowing with a birchbark winnowing basket. Everyone chuckles as they observe how difficult it is to keep the rice kernels from falling to the floor. Thelma turns the students' attention to significant ideas in the text by asking, "What spiritual meaning does the wild rice have?" Referring to her journal, Mandy offers, "It was a gift from the Creator." Thelma affirms Mandy's response and continues, "Why do they believe it was a gift from the Creator?" Carlos replies, "The Creator told them they would reach a place where food grew on the water." Thelma encourages everyone to reread the text which describes the spiritual nature of wild rice. After everyone agrees that Mandy's and Carlos' comments summarize the text, Thelma asks Hua to explain what food grows on the water. When Hua clarifies it is wild rice, Xee adds, "They [Ojibwa people] kept on going till they find their home in Minnesota and Wisconsin."

Ava works with five students in another literature circle. They examine an ear of corn similar to that grown in *Four Seasons of Corn: A Winnebago Tradition,*[2] the text they are reading. Both Charlotte and

7

Neal observe, "It's dried out." Jake adds, "You can get Indian corn at 'Little Farmer' [a local farm], but Europeans brought it up." Ava elaborates that her family also grew corn, but it was yellow and white, unlike the multicolored corn the Ho-Chunk grew. Ava asks, "Why do the Ho-Chunk people still grow corn? This family lived in the city. Was this a place where you can grow a lot of corn?" Denise adds, "The Great Spirit told the first person how to grow the corn and to keep it going. It's a food that's been around a long time. They don't want it to go away." Ava questions, "Remember when they started growing corn?" Charlotte says, "Since 1830," and Maria adds, "167 years." Ava repeats her question, "Why do they go to all this trouble?" Jake elaborates, "To keep history, to keep the spiritual corn thing going, their great-great-great-great-great-grandparents grew it."

BEGINNING OUR COLLABORATION

These scenes from Thelma's fourth-grade classroom came from our collaboration during the 1997-98 school year. It was a rare chance to teach with another experienced teacher, closely observe each other's teaching over a semester, and join our expertise in teaching state history for the benefit of fourth graders. Our goal was to provide rich learning opportunities for students by combining our content knowledge, instructional resources, and experiences with different teaching and assessment strategies. Figure 1–1 shows us in the midst of one of our many discussions. We developed and taught four multicultural Wisconsin history units during the fall semester of 1997-98 in Thelma's fourth-grade classroom:

1. Family History and the History of Different Cultural Groups Who Immigrated to Our State

2. Indigenous People's Traditional Lifestyle and Values Before Europeans; Changes and Hardships After European Contact

3. Development of State Government and Struggle for Voting Rights

4. Creation of State Industries

FIGURE 1–1 Thelma and Ava discuss their state history project in Thelma's classroom

For each unit, we incorporated the school district's fourth-grade social studies and literacy curriculum objectives and appropriate themes from *Expectations of Excellence: Curriculum Standards for Social Studies*.[3] These national standards were developed and published by the National Council for the Social Studies, the professional organization for social studies educators. At the time we taught the units, the standards for our state were not yet developed. After the state social studies standards were completed, which were largely based on the national standards, the school district aligned their curriculum objectives with the state standards. The state history units described within this text reflect current school district, state, and national standards. For each curriculum unit, we integrated:

- Multicultural ideas and themes[4]

- School district, state[5], and national social studies standards[6]

- Critical literacy[7]

9

- Social constructivist pedagogy[8]
- Culturally relevant teaching methods[9]
- Best teaching practices for social studies[10]

BUT I TEACH IN TEXAS;
WHAT DOES WISCONSIN HISTORY HAVE
TO DO WITH ME?

No matter where you teach in the United States, all states require the teaching of state history at the elementary level. When the National Council for the Social Studies developed a recommended scope and sequence for the social studies curriculum in 1989, they advised a study of regions in fourth grade. Often state legislatures mandate home state studies as one of the political regions.[11] However, the challenge for teachers who must teach about their own state is they must do so with limited teaching resources. Usually teachers rely on curricular materials created at the local or state level rather than from national publishers. Unfortunately, few elementary teachers have access to detailed social studies curriculum guides and instructional materials that are locally developed.[12] Because so few textbooks are available for teaching state history, teachers and school districts are faced with the challenge of creating curriculum appropriate for teaching state history. Although we focused on Wisconsin, our project offers ideas for a multicultural approach to teaching about different aspects of the history of any state. All state histories include:

- The indigenous people who first lived within the state

- Challenges, opportunities, and lifestyles of different cultural groups who immigrated into the state

- Conflicts among indigenous people, immigrants, and the U.S. government over land

- The creation of state government and the issue of which groups were extended voting rights and which groups were not

- The evolution of state industries based on the physical environment, technological changes, market needs, and workers' knowledge and skills.

BALANCING STANDARDS AND A MULTICULTURAL APPROACH

Multicultural Ideas and Themes

We were committed to a multicultural approach because we wanted to: emphasize the importance of all students' cultural backgrounds, including those cultures often neglected in the curriculum; provide equal opportunities for all children to learn; deal with examples of unequal treatment due to gender, race, and social class; and encourage our students to become advocates for equality in the world around them. Through a multicultural orientation to social studies, we believe that "teaching is our vehicle for making a difference in the world."[13] Because of our commitment to a multicultural approach, we wanted our social studies curriculum to address as many of Sleeter and Grant's[14] recommendations as possible regarding what should be included in the curriculum.

One suggestion is that the curriculum should deal with social issues such as racism, sexism, and classism. During our study of the formation of state government, we focused on the racism, sexism, and classism involved in decisions about who had voting rights at different times. Students questioned why women of any cultural group, and why Native Americans, African Americans, and European American men who did not own land could not vote in important decisions related to Wisconsin changing from a territory to a state.

Another recommendation is that the curriculum should integrate the experiences and perspectives of women and men from different cultural groups and include students' life experiences. For the family history unit, we focused on why Irish Americans, German Americans, Polish Americans, Mexican Americans, African Americans, and Hmong left their homelands and came to Wisconsin. At the same time, we encouraged students to make connections between these cultural groups and their own family histories. Students shared memories, activities, pictures, and artifacts from women, men, and children in their family histories.

A third suggestion for a multicultural curriculum involves encouraging students to think critically and analyze different perspectives. In our unit on Wisconsin Native nations, we used a variety of activities and resources to help students consider Native people's point of view regarding the fur trade, treaties, exercise of treaty rights, removal to reservations, and children's forced attendance at boarding schools. These perspectives were compared and contrasted to the goals of European fur traders and U.S. governmental representatives who negotiated treaties and removed Native people to reservations and boarding schools.

Finally, the curriculum should provide opportunities for students to become involved in social action projects, a challenging recommendation to follow! As we examined some of the prejudice and discrimination Native youth today experience as portrayed in trade books, we asked students to decide what actions they would take if Native American dancers came to our school to perform and members of the audience ridiculed them. Not only did students offer excellent ideas for welcoming and showing friendship to Native American guests and encouraging the audience to demonstrate acceptance of the dancers, but one of the Hmong girls shared similar experiences of being ridiculed on the school playground. We then discussed as a class how we can stand up for others who are being mistreated because of who they are.

School District, State, and National Standards

One of the reasons Thelma's school district agreed to allow us to do our collaborative project was our offer to incorporate the national social studies standards and the school district curriculum objectives in our curriculum. The school district social studies curriculum objectives were not yet aligned with national standards and the state social studies standards had not been created. In order to demonstrate that our curriculum met the recommendations for what should be taught in social studies by the National Council for the Social Studies, the main professional organization of social studies educators, we chose to integrate appropriate thematic strands within each unit. We especially liked the flexibility within the ten thematic strands in *Expectations of Excellence: Curriculum Standards for Social Studies*:[15]

1. Culture (groups create, learn, and adapt culture)

2. Time, Continuity, and Change (patterns of change and continuity within different cultures; diverse sources provide different historical perspectives; the past influences the present)

3. People, Places, and Environments (people adapt to and change their physical environments)

4. Individual Development and Identity (culture, groups, and institutions influence personal identity)

5. Individuals, Groups, and Institutions (institutions such as schools, churches, and families are formed and influenced by different factors; in turn they influence individuals and culture, and are maintained or changed)

6. Power, Authority, and Governance (people create, maintain, and change structures of power, authority, and government)

7. Production, Distribution, and Consumption (people produce, distribute, and consume goods and services)

8. Science, Technology, and Society (benefits and problems of technology and technological influences on society)

9. Global Connections (the balance of global interdependence and national interests in global issues such as health care, economic development, environment, and human rights)

10. Civic Ideals and Practices (ideals, principles, and practices of citizenship in a democratic republic; asks what does it mean to be a good citizen?)

These broad themes provided us with a great deal of flexibility in integrating them with multicultural ideas and themes. A number of the more specific performance expectations for each thematic strand were compatible with our multicultural approach.

Although the state social studies standards are based on the national standards, they define specific performance expectations for students by the end of grade four in five areas reflecting the main social science disciplines:

1. Geography: People, Places, and Environments

2. History: Time, Continuity, and Change

3. Political Science and Citizenship: Power, Authority, Governance, and Responsibility

4. Economics: Production, Distribution, Exchange, and Consumption

5. Behavioral Sciences: Individuals, Institutions, and Society (which include anthropology, psychology, and sociology).[16]

The state performance expectations for students are much more specific than the national ten thematic strands; however, the authors of the state guide, *Planning Curriculum in Social Studies*, encourage teachers to focus on big ideas and major concepts to help students gain "greater depth of knowledge and understanding."[17] This orientation also provided us with the flexibility to incorporate multicultural ideas into the state and national standards.

For the curriculum unit on "Indigenous People's Traditional Lifestyle and Values Before Europeans; Changes and Hardships After European Contact," we incorporated the Time, Continuity, and Change thematic strand. We focused on how Wisconsin Native people's lives changed over time because of contact with Europeans and European and Native American perspectives on different groups and events. Students worked in small cooperative groups to investigate Native people's traditional lifestyle or how they met their basic needs for food, clothing, and shelter before contact with Europeans. They learned about the traditional Native American value of taking only what you need to survive. Then we introduced the European fur traders who offered European products in exchange for furs. Students studied pictures and illustrations of trade goods, read about possible conflicts in cultural values and changes in Native people's lives resulting from trapping excessively to participate in the fur trade, and decided in their small groups if they believed it would be in the Native people's best interest to engage in the fur trade. Students tried to think as Native people in Wisconsin might have thought when they encountered European fur traders. This thematic strand also corresponded to the state and local school district performance expectations that our fourth-grade students would be able to: "explain the history, culture, and tribal status of the American Indian tribes and bands in Wisconsin"; "describe and distinguish among the values and beliefs of different groups or institutions"; and "investigate and explain similarities and differences in ways that cultures meet human needs."[18]

Potential Conflicts Between Multiculturalism and Standards

Although we found a great deal of flexibility to incorporate the national social studies thematic strands and state standards with our emphasis on multicultural state history, we were aware of some of the growing conflicts between many states' standards and multiculturalism. If state standards include very specific, detailed content, it becomes difficult for teachers to integrate diverse perspectives, various group's experiences, and build connections between their students' lives and the social studies curriculum.[19] Among the state history standards for fourth grade, we found the expectation that students will "examine biographies, stories, narratives, and folk tales to understand the lives of ordinary and extraordinary people, place them in time and context, and explain their relationship to important historical events"[20] supported our inclusion of diverse people in the curriculum, including the students themselves and their families. When we investigated why different cultural groups immigrated to Wisconsin, we encouraged the students to learn more about their family history and what led their families to move to Wisconsin. Several students interviewed members of their families and reported on what they learned to the class. One mother spoke to the class about the reasons for her family's emigration from India and immigration to Wisconsin.

A multicultural approach can also be undermined by standards which limit nontraditional materials and rely on textbooks with limited representations of diversity.[21] During our prior experiences in using textbooks, we found some students very interested in them and others very disengaged. They often do not represent everyone's cultural backgrounds and can make our Hmong, African American, and Mexican American students feel almost invisible. As a result, children become uninterested and unengaged in social studies. In this case, national standards are very compatible with a multicultural emphasis and promote the use of various resources for reconstructing the past.[22] One of the state standards explicitly encourages the use of diverse materials outside of traditional textbooks. "By the end of grade four students will identify and examine various sources of information that are used for constructing an understanding of the past, such as artifacts, documents, letters, diaries, maps, textbooks, photos, paintings, architecture, oral presentations, graphs, and charts."[23] During our family history unit, the students brought in many different resources to illustrate their own histories. The fourth graders shared photographs of current family members as well as those from generations past, important family artifacts such as a silver bowl, tatted handkerchief, and a family Bible, and precious documents, including several representing an ancestor's service in the Civil War.

Literacy and Critical Literacy

Literacy was also carefully integrated with our state history curriculum. We understood the benefits for students' learning when social studies was integrated with other disciplines, especially reading and language arts because students are reading and writing to learn social studies content. We reviewed the school district's literacy objectives and identified those appropriate for each curriculum unit. Both of us consulted reviews of trade books, then examined and identified trade books illustrating important ideas for the four main topics. We decided which we would use as whole class readings, literature circle, and other small group readings; which ones we would read aloud to the class, and which ones we would encourage students to read independently. In some cases, we had to create our own texts because we could not find appropriate published materials.

By integrating some of the school district's literacy objectives within the Indigenous Peoples unit, we anticipated students would:

• Use the index, table of contents, and glossary to gain information when reading expository text.

• Use a variety of comprehension strategies to gain meaning from complex text.

• Respond to reading through: role playing, writing logs, or journals; writing responses illustrating inferred meaning; explaining the author's purpose, character traits, and actions from different cultural perspectives; and summarizing expository text with main topic, main ideas, and supporting details.

• Select books of personal interest related to the curriculum unit and appropriate to their reading level.

Although we were dedicated to helping our students attain the basic literacy that is necessary for success in school and survival in society, we also wanted to incorporate critical literacy. By integrating critical literacy, we recognized the link between language and power and how our students' individual experiences as well as their gender, social class, and culture influenced their responses to texts and participation in discussions about readings.[24] In our teaching, that meant examining how domination is part of reading and writing, classroom interactions, and texts. For example, we tried to notice who talked the most in class discussions and whose ideas were listened to and discussed as indications of gender, class, and race privileges. We observed on numerous occasions that during whole class discussions, most of the contributions were made by boys from different cultural and social class backgrounds and a few European American girls. A number of girls from different cultural groups were more likely to be silent, offer fewer ideas, or their ideas were ignored by the class. In an effort to distribute students' power more equitably, we developed strategies to encourage contributions from more quiet students and emphasize their importance in class discussions.

Although we were dedicated to encouraging students to provide diverse interpretations of texts and exploring these in-depth, we also wanted to examine social issues suggested by texts, but ignored by students. For example, if students ignored such issues as sexism, racism, and classism, we raised these questions for students to discuss, but tried not to impose our own critique on students.[25] When we read about everyday life among nineteenth-century European American immigrants in *Little House in the Big Woods*,[26] we asked students to analyze the text for the significance of women's and men's contributions to family survival and for racist depictions of Native Americans. As we read, discussed, and critically analyzed texts, we encouraged students to search for verifiability of information, point of view, and bias; to compare texts written on the same issue or theme; and to develop a questioning attitude while reading.[27] This approach was especially appropriate during discussions of *Little House in the Big Woods* because the author wrote about her memories of living in Wisconsin many years after she experienced them. Students were invited to question the accuracy of the text based on the author's memories.

One way we encouraged critical literacy in the Indigenous Peoples curriculum unit was through the selection of texts which provided Native American perspectives on values, beliefs, and traditions. The texts were especially important to counteract some of the stereotypes, inaccuracies, and omissions in many published materials about Native people. Since Native Americans have a long history of oppression at the hands of European immigrants, European Americans, and the United States government, we hoped by providing authentic representations of the six Wisconsin Native nations that we could help erode some of the misunderstandings contributing to this oppression. During literature circle discussions we also encouraged the students to analyze the text to discover its accuracy, point of view, and bias by discovering who the authors were and examining their credentials for writing a book about Native people. Students were also invited to question why the main characters invested so much time in teaching, learning, and continuing their nation's traditions.

As we focused on incorporating critical literacy in Thelma's fourth-grade classroom, we kept three principles of critical literacy in mind.[28] First, that readers bring their own understanding of the world to whatever they read and, as teachers, we must help students make links between authors and themselves. For example, during the first curriculum unit, we discussed nineteenth-century immigrant family life as portrayed by the author in *Little House in the Big Woods* and asked students to compare the author's descriptions to their own family histories. Second, because readers bring personal meanings of social experiences to the text, no text has a single meaning. In our role as teachers, we encouraged students to make connections and respond to texts in a variety of ways to bring out these different meanings. During literature circle discussions of texts on Native Americans, we asked students to make personal connections with the main characters, including what they were learning about themselves as they learned about Ojibwa people participating in powwow traditions. A few students cited family members who sewed clothes for them or did other special deeds just as Ojibwa grandparents helped their grandchildren prepare powwow clothing. The four Hmong students believed the Hmong New Year clothing was similar to powwow clothing. Third, we acknowledged that students' voices are shaped by their experiences and cultural history, and provide the means for students to be heard and actively participate in the world. At times, this meant encouraging students to question their assumptions and interpretations of the readings. During the discussion of traditional powwow clothing, one of the European American boys said, "Americans don't wear traditional clothes unless it's Christmas time and they get dressed up to go out to eat." We encouraged the students to question who was included in the term "American." This led to a discussion about different cultural groups in the classroom who considered themselves "American" as well as Irish, Polish, German, Mexican, or Hmong.

Culturally Relevant, Social Constructivist Teaching Methods

Another component of our project was to use pedagogy which respected and built on students' prior knowledge and provided the greatest learning opportunities. We drew on both social constructivist pedagogy[29] and culturally relevant or culturally familiar teaching methods.[30] From our prior teaching experiences, we knew social constructivism was a valid learning theory because we observed students constructing understandings and influencing each other's learning. When students communicated what they were learning, it was not always what we believed we were teaching. Especially during group discussions, we observed students constructing shared meanings and interpretations through interactions with others, as shown in Figure 1–2. As teachers, our goal was to act as leaders, pose divergent questions, promote sustained and in-depth dialogue about a topic, elicit students' thinking, emphasize higher order thinking about authentic issues and problems, and share responsibility for learning with students. However, we agreed this approach did not mean an "anything goes" form of teaching and learning. Whenever students offered their interpretations of texts, we encouraged them to return to the texts to

FIGURE 1–2 Students often worked in small, cooperative groups to study state history

cite support for their explanations. We also modeled elaborating on our perspectives of texts with additional evidence and led students in critiquing the knowledge within the texts themselves.[31]

When Thelma discussed *The Sacred Harvest: Ojibway Wild Rice Gathering*[32] with a group of fourth graders, she asked them to refer to their texts for an explanation of reservations. She read aloud from the text, "The Ojibway were located in Minnesota, Wisconsin, Michigan, and North Dakota." Kay said, "It's a place where you live." Thelma probed, "Is where you live on Evans Street a reservation?" Kay responded, "No, it's where a bunch of people lived." Thelma again questioned, "Is Oshkosh a reservation?" Jacob interjected, "A reservation was where Indians took over the land or something." Thelma asked, "Did they really take over the land? How did they get this reservation, this place to live?" Carlos suggested, "In treaties, they set aside land." After Thelma elaborated on what reservations were, she asked the students to check the text for the name of the main character's reservation in Minnesota.

We appreciated social constructivism's recognition of the influence of the teachers' and students' cultural and social backgrounds on the knowledge we constructed together.[33] When we and our students entered the classroom, we recognized we each brought our cultural and social knowledge with us, which influenced the new knowledge we produced together. Consequently, we understood we needed to make our own cultural backgrounds more explicit rather than assume all students shared our culture; we needed to learn more about the children's cultural backgrounds and encourage students to share their cultures as part of the teaching and learning process.

By beginning with a unit on family history in which we and the fourth graders each described our own cultural backgrounds as part of our family history, we developed a basis for connecting each state history unit to our cultural and family backgrounds. As the students researched different cultural groups who immigrated to the state and investigated the creation of state government and industries, they made connections between their own families' immigration and participation in government and different industries. In addition, we recognized that when students shared their prior knowledge about a concept or topic, this knowledge may have been influenced by broader

21

cultural values such as individualism, competition, and materialism as well as sexism, racism, and classism, which are frequently reinforced by schools and society. When discussing early immigrant life in Wisconsin as represented in *Little House in the Big Woods*, we encouraged students to question their interpretations of the text based on the cultural values of individualism and male privilege. The fourth graders were asked to notice how the survival of the family depended on cooperation among all family members rather than the efforts of one individual. We asked them to note the importance of Ma's contributions as well as Pa's in providing food and clothing for their family.

Our teaching methods were also influenced by culturally relevant or culturally familiar pedagogy, which is similar to social constructivism. We built our teaching strategies on students' class, race, ethnic, and gender backgrounds and their prior knowledge, but also incorporated strategies congruent with students' cultural backgrounds in order to help students construct new knowledge. For example, some Native American cultures teach by children observing adults and by children and adults working cooperatively in completing a task. Latina/o cultural values include collectivism, interdependence, helpfulness, group success, and learning within the context of families.[34] Some African American students may come from a background that encourages public displays of emotions and simultaneous speech as they learn. Not only did we offer opportunities for students to use their preferred learning methods, but also to strengthen their abilities to use many different ways of learning.[35]

We were dedicated to becoming familiar with the students' cultural backgrounds and values and building on these in our teaching. Additionally, we wanted to attend to students' academic needs, especially children who have been less successful in school, such as our students from low socioeconomic levels, Hmong, and Mexican American backgrounds. We intended to use students' cultures as an avenue for learning, but we also planned to encourage students to critique values, such as individualism and competition, which perpetuated inequities.[36] For students whose cultural values include cooperation and group achievement (such as Latina/o and Hmong), we wanted to use cooperative learning as a culturally relevant teaching strategy.[37]

However, we were aware that some caution had to be used during cooperative learning. When students worked in small groups, we observed cooperative group work carefully to note the presence of low-status group members who talked less, were not listened to or taken seriously, handled the materials less, and at times were physically excluded.[38] We were aware that students' status was often determined by academic standing and popularity, although social class, race, and ethnicity may have also played a role. This became apparent in the family history unit when small groups of students investigated food-processing artifacts to learn more about immigrant life in Wisconsin during the late nineteenth century. As one group of four students questioned what the artifacts were and how they were used, every group member handled the butter churn, paddle, and butter mold and offered ideas except for one of the quiet Hmong girls. Hua was almost completely ignored and excluded from the discussion. She neither asked to manipulate the artifacts nor offered ideas, and no one in the group solicited her ideas or offered to share the artifacts with her. Until we viewed the videotape of this activity, we were unaware of Hua's limited participation in the small group. In future small cooperative group activities, we tried to avoid the harmful consequences of unequal participation in cooperative groups because less verbal, less involved students may learn less. We designed tasks necessitating multiple abilities and publicly praised the specific skills low-status students displayed in group tasks.[39] For example, one of the Hmong children with limited English often struggled with reading and writing in small group activities. However, when groups needed to summarize with drawings the results of their research, his art work was among the best. We openly praised his artistic contributions to the group and at the same time we provided additional help in reading and writing.

In order to provide opportunities for students to construct knowledge together during the Indigenous Peoples curriculum unit, we organized students into small, cooperative groups to investigate different characteristics of the six Native nations. Because six of the (nineteen) students were either Hmong or Mexican American, the small, cooperative groups were built on the Hmong and Mexican

American values of cooperation and group success over individual achievement.[40] Usually we encouraged students to decide which group members had the role of readers and writers. Readers were responsible for reading aloud from different sources and highlighting significant ideas while the writers recorded important ideas on paper. We worked with each group, encouraging all students to participate in either reading or recording ideas. We guided students in identifying main ideas and explaining these ideas in their own words. However, we asked students to fill different roles so everyone had the opportunity to read and write. Finally, each group cooperatively created drawings or charts to represent their main ideas to share with the class, which also required our guidance. For a couple of Hmong students who had limited English proficiency, we encouraged them to speak in their first language with other Hmong students as they completed their research and created their chart. Students drew on their different strengths in reading, writing, speaking, and drawing, but we expected everyone to use these different skills during small group research projects.

These small groups provided opportunities for observing how we helped students construct new knowledge based on prior understandings. As Ava worked with one group that was investigating the roles of women, men, elders, and children among a local Native American nation, the Stockbridge-Munsee, she noticed the students had difficulty finding information from their readings about what the children did. Ava encouraged the students to speculate about children's activities based on their prior research. Chia, Carlos, and John thought they might have carved objects from wood. Ava affirmed that idea and said there was plenty of wood to carve in the Stockbridge-Munsee's physical environment, but asked what they might carve. John suggested "Faces," while Chia added, "Shoes." Ava asked, "What kind of shoes did the Stockbridge-Munsee have?" Carlos quickly answered, "Moccasins." Ava continued, "What were they made from?" Chia, John, and Juan all said, "Deerskin." When Ava asked again, "What might they carve?" Chia offered, "Toys for them," and John thought "Tops." However, Carlos had a different idea, "They could carve what they think the Creator might look like." Ava responded, "I'm not sure about that. In some cultures, the Creator is considered too sacred to draw or carve. I'm not sure children would have the right to carve that kind of thing." John returns to the earlier idea of carving toys and Chia suggests "canoes." Ava affirms the quality of their thinking, "We don't know for sure, but it makes sense they would carve toy canoes." Chia, Carlos, and John continued to speculate about what Stockbridge-Munsee children might do for fun and the kinds of chores they might have in helping their families meet their basic needs. They drew on their earlier research of traditional foods, clothing, and shelter among the Stockbridge-Munsee to venture that children might help sew clothes, care for young children, cultivate a garden, and cover a wigwam or longhouse with bark.

Best Teaching Practices for Social Studies

By integrating many of the previous components in our approach to teaching state history, we were using many of the ideas identified as best educational practices for social studies education. However, we checked our teaching methods against the recommendations for "best practice" in social studies because we knew these came from the "most forward-looking ideas and arguments in the recent national reports, those most in touch with the research about children's learning and constructivist teaching, those most confirmed by the thinking and demonstrations and achievements we've observed in outstanding social studies classrooms."[41] It made sense to incorporate teaching practices which have been consistently shown to promote students' learning, such as:

1. Study topics in-depth and allow student choices of topics.

2. Use activities that engage students in inquiry and problem solving about significant human issues.

3. Form mixed ability groups and have students participate in interactive and cooperative study processes.

4. Integrate social studies with other areas of the curriculum.

5. Build on students' prior knowledge, study concepts from different social science disciplines, and develop richer content in elementary grades.

6. Explore a variety of cultures, including the students' own backgrounds.

Although our focus was on state history, we followed the best teaching practice of incorporating concepts from different social science disciplines, including history and geography in every curriculum unit, anthropology in units on family history and Native Americans, economics in the unit on state industries, and political science in the unit on state government. We tried to integrate as many of the five geographic themes as would be meaningful within each curriculum unit:

1. Location, or where a place is located on the earth's surface

2. Physical and human characteristics of a place

3. Human and environmental interactions, or how people modify and adapt to living in specific physical environments

4. Movement of people, goods, services, and ideas on the earth

5. Formation and changes of physical, political, and cultural regions.[42]

For example, when studying our state's indigenous people, students examined maps to identify where Native nations lived in Wisconsin during the early 1800s and where they live currently. We studied the effects of the physical environment on Native people's traditional lifestyles, identified regions of the world involved in the fur trade, and traced the movement of trade goods between Wisconsin and Europe during the fur trade era.

Another best teaching practice of integrating social studies with other areas of the curriculum justified inclusion of an important component of our project: literacy and critical literacy. Students read trade books in literature circles, we read trade books aloud, and as a class we read trade books to learn more about our state's history. By combining the instructional time for social studies with some of the time allocated for literacy instruction, we were able to focus on four, in-depth social studies units. Thelma arranged her daily schedule so we had blocks of teaching time two and one-half days a week.

Tuesday afternoons: 75 minutes

Wednesday mornings: 105 minutes

Wednesday afternoons: 50 minutes

Thursday mornings: 150 minutes

Thursday afternoons: 75 minutes

Finally, we integrated the practice of keeping students actively involved in learning and demonstrating their understandings by discussing, writing, dramatizing, and illustrating with drawings. We observed students' engagement with a variety of activities and students' explicitly communicated their preferences for specific methods of demonstrating what they learned. These strategies are also congruent with social constructivist, culturally relevant teaching methods.

PORTRAITS OF STATE HISTORY CURRICULUM IN ACTION

During the next four chapters we will describe important aspects of the four state history units we developed. Each chapter portrays our efforts to integrate standards, multicultural ideas, best teaching practices, and social constructivist, culturally relevant teaching methods. The closing of each chapter also includes our reflections on our teaching and students' learning and recommendations for creating your own state history curriculum. We hope you can learn from our experiences and apply some of our teaching strategies in your own classrooms. We were often pleased with students' engagement and learning, which told us we were using appropriate teaching methods to meet our students' needs and interests. However, we also discovered challenges with some of our content, teaching strategies, and resources. Our journey to create and teach multicultural state history is never ending.

ENDNOTES

1. Gordon Regguinti, *The Sacred Harvest: Ojibway Wild Rice Gathering* (Minneapolis, MN: Lerner, 1992).
2. Sally M. Hunter, *Four Seasons of Corn: A Winnebago Tradition* (Minneapolis, MN: Lerner, 1997).
3. National Council for the Social Studies, *Expectations of Excellence: Curriculum Standards for Social Studies* (Washington, DC: National Council for the Social Studies, 1994).
4. Christine A. Sleeter and Carl A. Grant, *Making Choices for Multicultural Education: Five Approaches to Race, Class, and Gender*, 3rd ed. (Upper Saddle River, NJ: Merrill, 1999), 188–216.
5. Hal Balsiger, Paula DeHart, Margaret A. Laughlin, Stephen A. Rose, and Michael Yell, *Planning Curriculum in Social Studies* (Madison, WI: Wisconsin Department of Public Instruction, 2001).
6. National Council for the Social Studies.
7. Donna C. Creighton, "Critical Literacy in the Elementary Classroom," *Language Arts* 74 (1997), 438–445; Carole Edelsky, "Education for Democracy," in JoBeth Allen, ed., *Class Actions: Teaching for Social Justice in Elementary and Middle School* (New York: Teachers College Press, 1999),147–156.
8. Jere Brophy and Janet Alleman, *Powerful Social Studies for Elementary Students* (New York: Harcourt Brace, 1996), 63–77; Geoffrey Scheurman, "From Behaviorist to Constructivist Teaching," *Social Education* 62 (1998), 6–9.
9. Gloria Ladson-Billings, "But That's Just Good Teaching! The Case for Culturally Relevant Pedagogy," *Theory Into Practice* 34 (1995), 159–165; Valerie O. Pang and Robertta H. Barba, "The Power of Culture: Building Culturally Affirming Instruction," in Carl A. Grant, ed., *Educating for Diversity: An Anthology of Multicultural Voices* (Boston: Allyn and Bacon, 1995), 341–358.
10. Steven Zemelman, Harvey Daniels, and Arthur Hyde, *Best Practice: New Standards for Teaching and Learning in America's Schools* (Portsmouth, NH: Heinemann, 1998), 132–155.

11. Task Force on Scope and Sequence, "In Search of a Scope and Sequence for Social Studies," *Social Education* 53 (1989), 376–385.
12. Brophy and Alleman, 19.
13. Sheldon Berman, "Educating for Social Responsibility," *Educational Leadership* 48, (1990), 75–80.
14. Sleeter and Grant, 188–216.
15. National Council for the Social Studies.
16. Balsiger et al.
17. Ibid., xi.
18. Ibid., 62, 116–117.
19. Anita P. Bohn and Christine E. Sleeter, "Multicultural Education and the Standards Movement: A Report from the Field," *Phi Delta Kappan* 82 (2000), 156–159; Michael Olneck, "Can Multicultural Education Change What Counts as Cultural Capital?" *American Educational Research Journal* 37 (2000), 317–348.
20. Balsiger et al., 61.
21. Bohn and Sleeter; Olneck, 332–337.
22. National Council for the Social Studies, 51.
23. Balsiger et al., 61.
24. Edelsky.
25. Ibid.
26. Laura Ingalls Wilder, *Little House in the Big Woods* (New York: HarperTrophy, 1971).
27. Creighton.
28. Ibid.
29. Brophy and Alleman, 63–77; Scheurman.
30. Ladson-Billings; Pang and Barba.
31. Brophy and Alleman, 63–77; Scheurman.
32. Regguinti.
33. Peter W. Airasian and Mary E. Walsh, "Constructivist Cautions," *Phi Delta Kappan* 78 (1997), 444–449.
34. Carrie Rothstein-Fisch, Patricia M. Greenfield and Elise Trumball, "Bridging Cultures with Classroom Strategies," *Educational Leadership* 56 (1999), 64–67.
35. Pang and Barba.
36. Ladson-Billings.
37. Sleeter and Grant, 188–216.
38. Elizabeth G. Cohen, "Making Cooperative Learning Equitable," *Educational Leadership* 56 (1998), 18–21.
39. Ibid.

40. Rothstein-Fisch et al.
41. Zemelman et al., 130.
42. Association of American Geographers and National Council for Geographic Education, *Guidelines for Geographic Education: Elementary and Secondary Schools* (Washington, DC: Association of American Geographers, 1984), 3–8.

CHAPTER 2

INTEGRATING FAMILY HISTORY
WITH STATE HISTORY

"It's important to know about others' family histories because if you think about it, all of our family histories are joined together."

(Mandy, fourth grader)[1]

Today students are sharing their family history projects with the rest of the class. We are pleased to discover everyone has completed a simple project by working on these at home with an adult member of their family. At the beginning of the school year, we met with at least one parent from each child's family to explain the different options the children could choose for their family history project and to request assistance as the student completed the project.

Maria, a Mexican American, stands in front of the class, and quietly explains parts of her father's Air Force uniform and the Vietnamese money he saved during his military service during the Vietnam War. She also reads from the transcript of an interview she had with her mother that revealed her mother's need for a job caused her to leave Mexico and settle in Wisconsin. From her family history timeline, Maria lists several events, especially the birth and death of her sister when her sister was very young. After listening carefully to Maria's presentation, class members question Maria about the reasons for her sister's death and discover a heart defect as the cause. Carlos asks which branch of the military Maria's father served in and Maria points to "Air Force" printed on the shirt.

Next, Jake, a Polish American, proudly shows many documents related to his great-great-great-grandfather who served in the Civil War and asks for our assistance in reading some of these documents.

When Jake shows copies of $13 to $15 paychecks for "fighting in the army," several class members comment on how small the amount is. We remind them that these amounts seemed much higher many years ago. Jake especially enjoys letting everyone know this relative was wounded by a bullet during the war that remained in his head for twenty-one days before being removed.

Rameen, whose family immigrated from India in 1992, smiles broadly and holds up a large poster with several pictures of his family arranged and labeled for everyone in the class to see. Although Rameen explains he is unable to read their Indian names, he points to the names of his maternal and paternal great-grandmothers and great-grandfathers on the chart and to photographs of family members participating in an Indian wedding in the United States. We elaborate that this special clothing is similar to the New Year clothing that Tong, Xee, Hua, and Chia wear when they attend the Hmong New Year celebration. Figure 2–1 shows Rameen as he reads from his paper on his family's history and elaborates that his family moved to this community from India because his uncle was already here, and they were able to find jobs in the area.

The class remains attentive while Hua, one of the four Hmong students, seriously explains her family tree and shows the class detailed pictures she has drawn of objects used or worn in Laos. One object, a basket, was used to carry corn and food and another sharp object, a weed cutter, was used to cut weeds when her family lived in Laos. The rest of the class found the bracelets the most fascinating as Hua explains they are used to "keep bad spirits away and have good luck." Several class members request additional information about the bracelets.

For the next two days, the students share family photographs and artifacts, family history timelines, summaries of interviews done with family members, and family trees. The class listens respectfully to each presentation and asks questions to learn more. These family history projects illustrate one of the goals we had for this unit, that the students would not only learn more about their own family history, but understand that their family history was connected to the different cultural groups who were part of our state's history and the significance of family history to the history of the state. Our goals re-

FIGURE 2–1 Rameen explains his family history poster

flected not only national and state standards, but recommended practices in multicultural and social studies education.

MANY PEOPLES, ONE STATE: INTEGRATING MULTICULTURAL IDEAS WITH STANDARDS

We began the first unit with a focus on diverse cultural groups, including the students' distinct cultures, that are part of the state's history. Native people from different nations were the first to live in our state. Then, immigrants from various parts of the world left their homelands for varied reasons and moved to the area, attracted by diverse aspects of the state. We inquired into the students' cultural backgrounds, then chose to focus on the most prevalent cultures represented by the fourth graders, which consisted of German Americans, Irish Americans, Polish Americans, Mexican Americans, and Hmong.[2] Although none were African American, we used trade books to introduce students to the history of involuntary immigration of African Americans to the United States and their eventual movement to our state. By focusing on diverse cultural groups within the state, we easily integrated national, state, and local school district standards with multicultural ideas.

School District, State, and National Standards

As we began our study of state history, we incorporated the national social studies thematic strand of Culture,[3] an important aspect of multicultural education and also part of the state and local social studies standards in the Behavioral Sciences. We wanted students to learn about their own cultural backgrounds as well as the backgrounds of others in the classroom. The specific state standard we addressed was:

• Students will investigate and explain similarities and differences in ways that cultures meet human needs.[4]

Geography was also integrated in the unit by addressing the thematic strand of People, Places, and Environments from the national standards. We hoped students would understand the effects of the physical and cultural environments of the immigrants' homelands that precipitated their emigration from their mother country and the attraction of Wisconsin's physical and cultural environments as a motivation for immigrating to the state. For the state standards, we expected our fourth graders to:

• Locate continents of the different homelands for each cultural group.

• Describe ways in which people interacted with the physical environment of their homelands and the state, including the use of land, location of communities, and design of shelters.

• Identify connections between the local community and other places in the state, the United States, and the world.[5]

The connection between state history and world history was another part of the curriculum and met the national thematic strand of

Global Connections and the state and local standards in Geography: People, Places, and Environments. We wanted students to understand that war or lack of economic opportunities in one part of the world led to the mass migration of some cultural groups to another part of the world. Specifically, we addressed the state standard:

• Students will identify connections between the local community and other places in Wisconsin, the United States, and the world.[6]

Because literacy was an important aspect of our state history curriculum, we concentrated on a few of the school district's literacy objectives. During the unit, fourth graders had opportunities to:

• Use a variety of comprehension strategies to gain meaning from more complex text.

• Summarize the main topic, main ideas, and supporting details of a text.

Multicultural Education

These standards were very compatible with the multicultural theme of the integration of the experiences and perspectives of different cultural groups, including the students themselves as members of these groups.[7] This theme was especially important to us because it makes students' cultural backgrounds an explicit part of the curriculum, making the curriculum relevant, meaningful, and engaging. If students make connections between themselves and what we are teaching, they are more likely to be engaged in their learning. We encouraged the fourth graders to develop a greater understanding of and appreciation for their own cultural identity, but also included African Americans, an important cultural group not represented among the students. We wanted to highlight the distinctions among Europeans who were voluntary immigrants from their homelands and came to the United States for a better life, Africans who were forced to leave their homes and enslaved in the United States, and Hmong who escaped from war in their homeland and moved to the United States as refugees.

Critical Literacy

Critical literacy involves students and teachers examining texts for point of view, bias, and issues of justice and injustice. It means making connections between texts and diverse students' lives, and addressing issues of fairness in who speaks and is listened to during discussions.[8] Critical literacy was incorporated through the use of trade books to illustrate diverse perspectives on why groups left their homelands and came to the United States and our state and to raise the social issue of slavery for the fourth graders to discuss. As we discussed the texts with students, the fourth graders were encouraged to make personal connections between the texts and themselves and explain their different points of view. When reading aloud *Coming to America: The Story of Immigration*[9] to the class, we asked the students to compare their own families' immigration experiences with the immigrant experiences described in the text. We also encouraged students to question the text by introducing many Native people's belief that they originated in the Americas rather than immigrated from Asia.

SMALL GROUP RESEARCH: BEST PRACTICES AND CULTURALLY RELEVANT, SOCIAL CONSTRUCTIVIST METHODS

We asked students to research the homelands of their families, then divided students into small groups of three or four based on the most common cultural backgrounds. Because we wanted students to work together cooperatively to complete research, those individuals who claimed Russian, Italian, and Indian ancestry worked with students who came from more prevalent cultural groups, including German, Polish, Irish, Mexican, and Hmong. They investigated reasons why a cultural group left their homeland and what attracted them to the state. By encouraging students to work in small groups to learn about diverse cultures in state history, we followed two specific recommendations for the best teaching practices for social studies:

• Explore a variety of cultures, including the students' own backgrounds.

• Form mixed ability groups and have students participate in interactive and cooperative study processes.[10]

This small group activity provided opportunities for the fourth graders to gather information and construct knowledge together, a significant aspect of social constructivism. It also used the culturally relevant teaching method of building on students' cultural values, such as the traditional Hmong and Mexican American cultural value of cooperation.[11] We especially wanted to emphasize cooperation over the traditional European American value of individualism to support the academic achievement of our Hmong and Mexican American students.

Supporting English Language Learners

For this research project, we placed the four Hmong students, Hua, Xee, Chia, and Tong, into one group to investigate Hmong emigration from Laos and immigration to the United States in the belief that they would find the topic more interesting and engaging since it was similar to their own families' experiences. In order to support their success with this challenging task, we provided a picture book that added important visual aids and encouraged the students to discuss what they were learning in Hmong as well as English. Although we did not usually place all four Hmong students in one group during our state history activities, we used several strategies to promote the academic achievement of Chia and Tong, who were still learning English and participated in the English as a Second Language program. We always held them to the same high expectations as all other fourth graders, but provided additional support so they could meet those expectations. One strategy was to frequently place Chia or Tong, who were still developing skills in speaking, reading, and writing English, in a group with either Hua or Xee, who had more developed English skills. We encouraged the Hmong students to help one another during individual and group activities, including talking over ideas in Hmong and English, but did not ask Hua and Xee to spend too much time providing assistance. Although neither of us nor Kristen, our research assistant, spoke Hmong, we consistently provided additional support for Tong and Chia. We read difficult texts with them, discussed the meanings of the readings, asked them to summarize what they were learning, and assisted with writing their ideas. At the beginning of the semester, Tong dictated what he wanted to write to one of us who recorded it on the board. Tong then copied it. By the end of the semester, Tong was writing more independently.

Including African American Involuntary Immigration

Because we did not have any African American students in the class, we introduced the story of Africans' involuntary immigration to the United States through the picture book *Now Let Me Fly: The Story of a Slave Family*.[12] The text allowed us to raise briefly the injustices of slavery with the class. We read aloud part of the text that illustrated the capture of a young African girl named Minna in 1815, her forced march to the coast, travel on a crowded ship, sale to slave owners in the United States, and the harsh work in cotton fields as a slave. The picture book *The Great Migration: An American Story*[13] represented reasons why African Americans left the South and moved to northern cities such as Milwaukee and Chicago during World War I. Following the reading, main ideas were summarized on a chart with the headings: "Why African Americans left their homeland" and "Why African Americans came to our state" as a model for students to follow in their own small group research.

Beginning Small Group Research

Because this was our first small group activity for the year, we discovered the fourth graders were challenged to work with other group members cooperatively. At times students argued with one another, were off task, and not all actively participated. With the two of us and Kristen, our research assistant, helping groups work together, the fourth graders were eventually able to complete the task and each student learned from it.

In each group, students chose who served as readers and writers during the research process. Readers read aloud from the resources while writers took notes. At first we provided issues of *Badger History*, a state history magazine published by the State Historical Society of Wisconsin for elementary students, as a secondary source of information on Mexican Americans, German Americans, Polish Americans, and Irish Americans, but discovered these were too difficult and time consuming for many of the students to use. We then created our own summaries of main ideas from these magazines, which were more accessible to the students, although significantly condensed, as shown in Figure 2–2.

For the Hmong students' investigation of Hmong migration from Laos to our state, we provided them with the picture book *Dia's Story Cloth*[14] as a source of information. This book was especially helpful for the Hmong students with limited reading skills because it was well-illustrated with photographs of a story cloth depicting the war in Laos and the escape of the Hmong to Thailand and eventually to the United States. With the visual clues from the text, the discussion of main ideas in Hmong and English, and additional assistance from one of us, the Hmong students completed this task successfully.

With our guidance, the students gathered main ideas from printed, secondary sources. The fourth graders cooperatively created a visual representation in words and pictures of their understanding of the main reasons for their group's migration from their homeland to Wisconsin and explained it to the class.

Escape from Oppression and Limited Economic Opportunities: Polish Americans

The students worked in small groups around the classroom illustrating what they learned from their small group research about why different cultural groups left their homelands and immigrated to our state. Sometimes group members looked at the notes they recorded from the research, sometimes we reminded them to review their notes. Jacob, Judy, John, and Jake gathered around their chart paper, but each drew a different picture to illustrate reasons for leaving Poland and moving to Wisconsin during 1870–1910. One drew a picture of the German

MEXICAN IMMIGRANTS IN WISCONSIN

Why did Mexicans leave their homeland of Mexico?

Many Mexican people did not find ways to earn enough money to live in Mexico. They came from small farms that did not produce enough food to feed their large family or they had to live on farms which belonged to someone else.

Mexican farm workers earned little pay and often were not able to go to school. More schools are being built in the rural areas of Mexico, but many children are unable to attend these schools because they are needed to help with the farm work.

Why did Mexicans come to Wisconsin?

People who needed to hire workers went to Mexico during the 1920s to encourage Mexicans to come to Milwaukee and work in factories. Mexicans were promised they would have steady work and a good wage if they came to Milwaukee.

During World War II, workers from Mexico were encouraged to come to Wisconsin to harvest crops because so many men were away fighting in the war. Mexicans from Mexico and Mexican Americans already living in the southwest came to Wisconsin during World War II to harvest crops and stayed to work in factories. Now more Mexicans work in factories than on farms.

Young men may come to Wisconsin to work and earn money so they can send it home to help their families in Mexico.

After the first Mexicans came to Wisconsin, other Mexicans knew they could come to Wisconsin and stay with relatives while they looked for jobs.

FIGURE 2–2 Original text we created explaining Mexican immigration to our state

leader Bismarck saying "You can't speak Polish," another illustrated money, someone else drew a small house on a small piece of land to depict the reasons motivating Poles to leave their homeland and settle in Wisconsin. They added an outline of our state to their chart and included a picture of a larger farm and railroad tracks to represent the appeal of more land and jobs with the railroad to draw Polish people to the state.

During individual interviews at the end of the unit, all four students could explain why Poles left their homeland. They knew that limited income and farmland and the lack of freedom to practice their religion and speak their language motivated Poles to leave Poland. They also knew Poles were attracted to our state by the better jobs, inexpensive farmland, and low taxes. In particular, Jake elaborated on the encouragement from Polish friends and relatives who already had immigrated to Wisconsin as a motivation for Poles to leave their homeland and settle near them in the "new country." However, he had developed an exaggerated notion of the number of Poles who settled in this area. "The Poles moved over here and heard there was farmland in the state, so they moved here and told other people about it and more people came and more people came until most of the Poles are here [*sic*]."[15]

Economic and Political Motivations for Immigration: German Americans

Charlotte, Denise, Susan, and Neal investigated reasons for Germans to leave Germany and settle in Wisconsin from 1840 through the early 1900s. They created a chart (see Figure 2–3) with many ideas, but emphasized the economic motivations with illustrations of small amounts of money in Germany and larger amounts in Wisconsin.

During the interviews, each member of the group was able to explain why Germans left their homeland and settled in the state. They cited low-paying jobs, limited farmland, and the desire to be free from their restrictive government and practice their own religion as motivations for leaving Germany. They also elaborated on why German immigrants were attracted to the state: better farmland, better

WHY GERMANS LEFT HOMELAND	WHY THEY CAME TO OUR STATE
Germans wanted freedom from their leaders	Germans wanted freedom from their leader
They came because of religion	They came for cheap farmland
They got more land	Better opportunities
Jobs paid less money	So they can vote
Didn't want to serve in army	Wanted to be citizens
They had to pay more money [for food, clothing, and shelter]	Jobs paid more to pay lower taxes
	Got to live closer to people to start their own things

FIGURE 2–3 Student chart

paying jobs, and the freedom to start their own schools and churches. Charlotte explained these ideas well:

> Germans came because their leader [Bismarck] was mean, and they wanted to get away from him. He didn't let them do their own parishes [practice their own religion]. He wanted them to be under his rule. They got less money there in the factories. They worked so hard for little money. They came here for better money, for the good farmland that was here. They heard about how good job opportunities were around here.[16]

Search for Greater Economic Opportunities: Irish Americans

Kay, Patty, Mandy, and Danny focused on Irish Americans' reasons for leaving their homeland and settling in the state from 1840 to 1920. For their chart, they drew an illustration of a limp potato plant with small potatoes on the vine as the motivation to leave Ireland. A drawing of a potato plant with large potatoes growing on it embellished their reasons for settling in Wisconsin. During the individual end-of-the-unit interviews with the fourth graders, each understood that the potato famine and lack of jobs, income, and food led to the movement of many Irish people from their homeland to the United States. The students also explained that Irish Americans were attracted to the state's good, inexpensive farmland, which provided food and job possibilities. Mandy summarized:

> They left their homeland because of the potato famine. Many people starved and died from disease. They came to the state because they heard there was better food and crops and it didn't cost that much money to make [crops] and they could be free from English rule.[17]

Pursuit of Better Economic and Educational Opportunities: Mexican Americans

Rameen, Carlos, and Maria focused on Mexican Americans' reasons for leaving their homeland and immigrating into the region beginning in the 1920s through World War II to now. They illustrated the reasons for emigrating from Mexico with the Mexican flag and an outline of Mexico and the motivations for immigrating to Wisconsin with the U.S. flag and an incomplete outline of Wisconsin, as shown in Figure 2–4. By the end-of-the-unit interviews with the students, each was able to explain the lack of good jobs, little farmland, limited income to support their families, and few educational opportunities for their children as being the impetus for emigrating from Mexico. They also learned that Mexicans were drawn to the state due to job possibilities, higher wages, and better educational prospects. Carlos, whose family came from Mexico, elaborated:

> Mexican Americans came to Wisconsin to get jobs and plant sugar beets and to have a better life and to get more money. And they left Mexico because they needed more farmland to support their families and most of the farmland was bought. Some kids could get an education because there were schools in Mexico, but they were usually far away and they usually had to stay home and help with the farmland.[18]

43

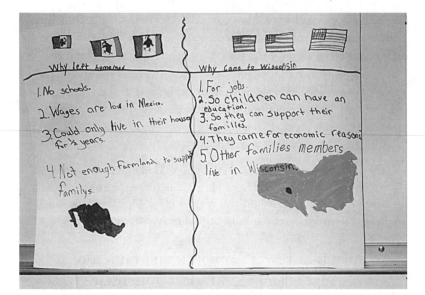

FIGURE 2–4 Chart summarizing cooperative group research on Mexican immigration to Wisconsin

Escape from War: Hmong

In another group, Hua, Chia, Xee, and Tong discussed in Hmong what they should draw on their chart. They used the same book for their chart as they did for their research, *Dia's Story Cloth*.[19] Chia looked carefully at the illustrations and drew houses in Laos, then added planes dropping bombs on the houses. Tong worked meticulously to complete a detailed illustration of a jet that took the Hmong from refugee camps in Thailand to the United States. They decided to use words to show their ideas and they wrote the following caption under the heading "Why Left Homeland:" "Soldiers fighting in Laos. They were not in safety. Can't cook because the fire would light the part they are on. Couldn't grow food." On the second half of their chart, they wrote the heading "Why came to Wisconsin?" and added, "They came to find a job and freedom. Churches offered to help them to come to Wisconsin. Relatives sponsored them. So they can get an education."

During the end-of-the-unit individual interviews, the four Hmong students were able to explain that war was the main reason for the migration of Hmong people from Laos. Although Tong often struggled to explain his ideas in English, he had a grasp of the impetus for the move. "They have to leave because there was a war in Laos. If they didn't leave they would die. They didn't like to live there because they were scared. There was a lot of people over there and there was bad soldiers were trying to shoot them."[20] These four students also listed the cultural advantages of assistance from Lutheran churches, relatives already living in the area, and educational opportunities as providing further motivations for Hmong people to move to Wisconsin.

FOCUS ON YOUR STATE: INVESTIGATING DIFFERENT CULTURAL GROUPS

In order to gather background information on different cultural groups living in your state for your own state history curriculum, you might:

• Survey your students' families to discover their cultural backgrounds and the homelands from which their ancestors came. For Native American students and families, inquire into the Native nations to which the families belong and the longevity of those nations' presence in your state.

• Contact the local museum, public library, and historical society for background information and such teaching resources as books and other print documents, photographs, artifacts, videos, websites, guest speakers, and field trips to help teach about the main cultural groups living in your area. You might investigate why the groups emigrated from their homelands and what attracted them to your area.

• Contact the state historical society, Native American tribal offices and reservations in your state, and your department of public instruction for background information and teaching resources on your state's primary cultural groups, motivations for each group to leave their homeland, and the reasons for their settlement in your state. For more information about which Native American nations live in your state, see *www.nativeamericanonline.com.*

• Contact local human service organizations that support immigrants or refugees, such as the Hmong-Lao Association, for information on current immigrants and refugees in your state and the factors precipitating their emigration from their homeland to your state.

FAMILY HISTORIES: MAKING STATE HISTORY PERSONAL

At the same time students worked in small groups to investigate different cultural groups who left their homelands and came to our state for various reasons, they researched their own family histories. We wanted the fourth graders to learn more about their family's history, connect their family history with the history of different cultural groups who immigrated to Wisconsin, and understand that family history is a significant aspect of state history. Through informal discussions, we discovered that none of the students were of Native American descent. Then we met with a member of each fourth grader's family to explain the family history project options. The conferences were followed by a letter to the students' families asking them to talk with their children about why their family left their homeland and moved to this part of the United States. A copy of the letter is shown in Figure 2–5. As the students discovered reasons for their families' emigration from their homelands and settlement in the state, we encouraged the fourth graders to discover similar motivations for different cultural groups to move to Wisconsin.

The gender, social class, and cultural diversity among the students enriched the multicultural curriculum. As the fourth graders investigated their family histories, they used diverse resources, including artifacts and family members who were knowledgeable of family history. Each student had help from someone in her or his family in completing the research. The families also served as resources to the class by serving as guest speakers to portray different perspectives and experiences on family history.

Dear Family,

We would like for the children in our class to learn more about their family histories as we learn about Wisconsin history. We are asking for your help. Please discuss the following questions with your child. You may find that you do not know the answers to all questions, but please share whatever information with which you feel comfortable.

> What was my family's homeland before living in Wisconsin?
> Why did my family leave their homeland?
> When did they leave?
> Why did my family move to Wisconsin?
> Where did they settle? Why?
> What has kept my family in Wisconsin?

One of the assignments for this unit will require the children to choose one of the following four activities to share with the class. The children will need to share what they learned about their family history through the activity.

1. Interview a relative who is knowledgeable about family history.
2. Complete a family chart or tree showing the child, parents, and grandparents.
3. Complete a family history timeline showing when important events happened in your family's history. You might begin with the present and go back as far as you can, focusing on the decades 1990, 1980, 1970, 1960, and so forth.
4. Learn more about significant family artifacts or objects which are important in your family. These may include a pair of old baby shoes, old letters, photograph albums, family quilt, story cloth, baptismal gowns, or toys.

In addition, we invite *you* to be a guest speaker for the class. You might share a part of your family history through pictures, artifacts, stories, story cloths, family history quilts, or other family history documents. Please let us know as soon as possible if you would be available to be a guest speaker so we can schedule your visit before September 25.

Thank you for the help you have given your child in learning more about her or his family history. Please contact us if you have any questions.

Sincerely,

Mrs. Ristow   Dr. McCall

FIGURE 2–5 Letter sent to students' families about the family history project

Meeting Standards, Multicultural Ideas, and Best Teaching Practices

Our focus on family history met the multicultural theme of including the experiences and perspectives of several different cultural groups,[21] and the best teaching practices of building on students' prior knowledge, studying concepts from different social science disciplines, and exploring a variety of cultures, including the students' own backgrounds.[22] Because of our emphasis on using diverse resources in researching family history, we also incorporated the Time, Continuity, and Change thematic strand and similar state standards. Specifically, we provided opportunities for our fourth graders to:

• Identify and examine various sources of information that are used for constructing an understanding of the past.

• Examine stories and narratives to understand the lives of ordinary and extraordinary people, place them in time and context, and explain their relationship to important historical events.

• Identify and describe significant events and people in the history of Wisconsin and the United States.

• Describe examples of cooperation and interdependence among individuals and groups.[23]

When students prepared a written summary of their family history for a class book, we also addressed one of the school district's literacy objectives. The fourth graders were able to:

• Use the writing process to prepare their writing for publication.

Investigating and Sharing Family Histories: Students and Families As Resources

At the beginning of the semester, we met face to face with each family to explain the family history project. For Hmong parents with limited English-speaking skills, we invited the English as a Second Language

Hmong interpreter to attend the conference and interpret our explanation of the family history project from English to Hmong and the parents' questions and responses from Hmong to English. These meetings were instrumental in allowing each child to complete a project successfully and gain additional knowledge of the family's history. During this initial conference, we explained four different options their children could use to explore their family history:

1. Interview a relative about family history and summarize what was learned.

2. Complete a family chart or tree.

3. Develop a family history timeline.

4. Learn more about important family artifacts or objects.

Because we recognized the sensitive nature of family history projects, we reassured family members their child should investigate only what families felt comfortable sharing about their family history. During the conferences, a few family members expressed their concern about not having enough knowledge to help their child complete a project successfully. However, we assured them that whatever knowledge they had would be enough.

Our invitation to family members to participate in the unit by serving as guest speakers about their family history led to additional learning opportunities for all the fourth graders to discover different experiences and perspectives on family history. Two mothers from European American backgrounds (German and Polish) shared with the class old family photographs or artifacts, such as a silver bowl and serving spoons that had been passed down in the family for over 100 years. Rameen's mother served as a guest speaker explaining why her family left India and moved to Wisconsin in 1992. She emphasized women's limited power in India to choose their own spouses, visit their biological families after marriage, and work outside the home. She described the challenges of leaving their successful businesses, moving to the United States, learning English, and finding jobs. However, she and her family were motivated to move to find better educational opportunities for their children.

When students presented their family history projects to the class, they explained and showed family artifacts such as dishes, tatted handkerchiefs, a photograph of a great-great-grandmother, family trees, and a timeline of important events in their family from 1920 until the present. Several summarized a report of what they learned about their family history from talking with family members. Students' class presentations of their family history projects, which were videotaped and listened to carefully by the other fourth graders, were excellent learning opportunities for students. Not only did all fourth graders increase their understanding of their own family history, but their knowledge of other students' family history was also enriched. Following each child's presentation, the rest of the class asked questions, which illustrated their interest in the presentation and allowed the presenters to elaborate on an aspect of their family history. When the Hmong students described their families' escape from Laos after the Vietnam War, we elaborated on why many Hmong people chose to leave Laos, live temporarily in refugee camps in Thailand, and eventually settle in the United States and Wisconsin. We wanted all the fourth graders to understand how the Hmong assisted the United States during the war in exchange for the promise to be taken care of by the U.S. government after the war.

During individual interviews at the end of the unit, it was obvious that all students increased their knowledge about their family history. They understood what countries their ancestors emigrated from; why they emigrated; how they traveled to the United States; where they first settled in the United States; why they moved to the state; special artifacts used or kept in their family; the lifestyle of their ancestors; and family members' war activities or notable occupations.

Carlos explained what he learned about his family's migration from Mexico to the United States:

> I didn't know my grandpa was a writer in Mexico. I thought my great-grandpa said that my grandpa could go [to America], but he didn't want him to go. He wanted him to stay in Mexico. My grandpa went to save money.[24]

By the end of the unit, nearly all students learned about others' family histories. During the interviews, they explained that families came from diverse countries; some families came to the United States because of war; ancestors had distinct occupations and participated in different wars; families had special artifacts; family members lived in the same city; and a street in the community was named after one family. Jake explained what he learned about the Hmong New Year from listening to the Hmong students' presentations on their family history:

> Hmongs have a special tradition, Hmong New Year. They got a special costume they wear, it's hand stitched. Sometimes they have little stitches in the back or else they have that part holding down in the back [a collar with decorative stitching]. I think that is hard work [to sew], probably four or five weeks, I mean months, four or five weeks, that would be a miracle![25]

We created a class book of our family histories by compiling written summaries from each student of what they learned. The students were excited to receive their own copy of the book and quickly found their family history within it. Hua summed up her family history for the class book:

> My maternal mother and father's names are __ and my mom's dad's name is __. They both got married in Laos. My mom's dad died in Laos. My mom's dad's brothers became soldiers in Laos. My mom was also born in Laos. My mom's dad died in the water in Laos. My paternal dad's name is __ and my dad's mom's name is __. They both got born in Laos. My dad's mom and dad got married in Laos. My dad also was born in Laos.
>
> My mom said she used to have a cat in Laos and also a dog, but her cat died in Laos. My mom was born in 1963. My dad was born in 1957. They both got married in 1982. My dad once had a cow, but once my mom was feeding it food and the gate was opened. It ran wild and got out. It ran all over the place, but then they caught the cow.
>
> When they went to their garden they would take a weed cutter and a basket. They take the basket for food and crops and the weed cutter is for cutting weed. They traveled a very long way. In Laos, my mom's sister and she wore the silver bracelets and the red bracelets.
>
> It was a very long trip for them because they traveled a lot of states, to come to America. They traveled to Thailand. Then my big sister was born. There was a war in Laos so they came to Thailand then America. It was hard for my mom, dad, and my sister.

We hoped students would understand the importance of family history in the context of state history. As the students made their family history presentations, we emphasized the significance of their family's contributions to our state and similarities between their families' movement to the state and motivations for diverse cultural groups' immigration to Wisconsin throughout the state's history. However, this generalization that family history was connected to state history was very challenging. Most students did not demonstrate this understanding during the individual interviews at the end of the unit. For those few who grasped that ordinary people like themselves helped to shape state history, they offered significant ideas: "Because the state was brought up from a whole bunch of different people";[26] "Because some of their families, like Jake, had people in his family that were important and got—like—streets named after them";[27] and "A person's family history is important to state history because what they did is probably something everybody wants to remember."[28] Mandy expressed her understanding of the connection among everyone's family histories that necessitated learning about them:

> Because if you think about it, and go from generation to generation to generation, we're all kind of connected as a whole family. So other people's family history is actually part of yours, too. So if you remember that, the part you don't remember, you're probably even losing some of your own family history.[29]

FOCUS ON YOUR STATE: INTEGRATING FAMILY HISTORIES WITH YOUR STATE HISTORY

In order to invite participation from and show sensitivity to diverse families as you integrate family history with your state history curriculum, you might:

• Offer different options to allow for children of single parent, blended, adopted, and foster families to complete a family history project. If possible, meet with each family to explain the project and to respond to families' questions and concerns.

• For families who are reluctant to share their family histories, you might arrange alternative projects, such as investigating the family history of a member of the school community (volunteer, another teacher, secretary, or custodian).

• Encourage your students to investigate reasons for their families' presence in your state, what life was like in your state during earlier periods of time, different jobs and volunteer activities family members held in your state, and contributions their families made to your state.

• Explore different family history resources for additional guidance in integrating family history projects with your state history. You might contact the local genealogical society, the local historical society, the public library, and Native American nations in your area for teaching resources and elders or other guest speakers who could assist in your students' family history research. Valuable resources and guidelines are also offered in *Do People Grow on Family Trees? Genealogy for Kids & Other Beginners* and *Through the Eyes of Your Ancestors: A Step-by-Step Guide to Uncovering Your Family's History.*[30]

IMMIGRATION EXPERIENCES: UNDERSTANDING AND EMPATHIZING

After the students completed their small group research on different cultural groups who settled in our state and their family history projects, we wanted them to understand the challenges for European immigrants entering the United States through such entry points as Ellis Island. Here immigrants endured humiliating health inspections and personal questions about marital status, prior education, and employment history. If family members had communicable diseases, they were forced to stay in a quarantine section of Ellis Island until the ill member recovered. For those immigrants diagnosed with incurable diseases, such as trachoma, they were not allowed to enter the United States and were forced to return to their homeland. The remaining family members had to decide if they would return to their homeland, too, or enter the United States without the ill family member.

In order to help students understand and empathize with immigrants' experiences, we used a simulation about the passage of three families through Ellis Island. Although our focus was on European immigrants rather than immigrants from many different parts of the world, we addressed national, state, and local school district standards and recommended practices in social studies teaching.

Meeting Standards, Social Constructivist Teaching Methods, and Best Teaching Practices

The Ellis Island simulation enabled students to understand more about European immigrants' experiences, vulnerabilities, and limited rights as they entered the United States during the late nineteenth and early twentieth centuries. Our goals matched the Time, Continuity, and Change national thematic strand that emphasized how people viewed themselves during different time periods.[31] We also addressed the corresponding state and local school district standard by providing opportunities for our students to:

• Compare and contrast contemporary life with life in the past, looking at social, economic, political, and cultural roles played by individuals and groups.[32]

Through our small group discussions during the simulation and the whole class discussion following it, we used an important aspect of social constructivism.[33] We provided opportunities for students to build knowledge about the different experiences and feelings European immigrants might have had when they entered the United States through Ellis Island during the nineteenth and early twentieth centuries. The simulation is the type of activity recommended as a best teaching practice in which students participate in interactive and cooperative study processes and mixed ability groups.[34]

Simulations: A Glimpse into Immigrants' Experiences

Kristen, our research assistant, significantly modified a published Ellis Island simulation, "Gateway"[35] for a one-hour activity. We drew on additional background knowledge from other texts[36] to guide three different immigrant families' movements through Ellis Island. We hoped students would learn about many immigrants' experiences of entering the United States and passing inspection points regarding their health, character, and vocation. For the Ellis Island simulation, each student drew a colored card with an identity written simply as "mother," "father," "child," "aunt," or "uncle." All students with the same colored card became members of one family immigrating to the United States. When the family members first entered the classroom, the three of us asked the fourth graders to form a line for their health inspection. We asked all families questions about their eyesight and hearing, examined their heads, arms, and hands for rashes, and checked their eyes for any diseases. Without explaining our actions, we placed masking tape on the clothing of a few new immigrants to identify those as having communicable, but curable diseases and a few more as having contagious, incurable diseases.

All the members of one family were judged physically healthy and Kristen led them to a table in the classroom designated as the character station. There, she asked the adult family members such questions as: "Have you ever been in jail? Have you ever been divorced? Do you belong to any political parties or organizations in your native country? Do you have $30 in your possession?" If their answers illustrated "good" character and the financial resources to travel to their destination, Kristen then guided them to another table in the classroom identified as the vocation station. Here she inquired about the adults' educational levels, job skills, and employment records to determine if the new immigrants would be able to support themselves and their families economically in the United States. After "passing" this station, the family went to the "Welcome to America" section of the classroom. Here they discussed and recorded in their journals their feelings about being successful in completing the journey to the United States, how other families might feel who were not successful in passing through Ellis Island, what the markings on clothing might mean, and what they might do after they leave Ellis Island. After successfully passing all the stations with her family, Susan wrote in her journal: "It was ese to get to Amarica. It was also hard. You had to ancer all the quastions and Neal almost didn't mack it." Patty's journal illustrated some of the uncertainties she experienced:

> When I went through Elis Island, I felt scard and I wonderd if I was going to make it or not. I wonderd if my husband would make it and not I. I also wonderd if I would make it and not my husband or my child. I didn't smile the hole day, not even a grin. I didn't know what was going on. I hardly knew how to speak English. I mostly just spoke Irish.

After identifying a few members of the second family as having a contagious, but curable "rash" and marking their clothing, Thelma directed this family to the quarantine area of the classroom. While they waited for the "rash" to heal, Thelma asked them to discuss and record in their journals their feelings about being in quarantine, what they might do if they could continue through Ellis Island and enter the United States, and what they might do if they could *not* continue through Ellis Island and enter the United States. Following a short time in quarantine, Thelma then led this immigrant family through the character and vocation stations. Judy elaborated on her experiences and feelings in her journal: "Being a member of the yellow family was scary. We all had something rong with us. The mother and one of the children allmost had to go back but they clard [cleared]." Maria also recorded concerns about her family in her journal: "Today I played an uncle. I thought that some of my (fake) family were going back. And I was nervous because Mrs. Ristow was asking questions that I didn't understand."

The third family had a few members with a contagious and incurable disease. Ava guided this family to the "Return to Homeland" table in the classroom to discuss possible options. They had to decide if just those family members with the disease would return to their homeland or if the entire family would return. They needed to consider what was best for the entire family, including the healthy members and those with the disease. Students discussed their feelings about this dilemma, voiced their recommendations about what they should do, and recorded their ideas in their journals. Denise, in the role of a child who returned to her homeland with her mother, wrote in her journal: "I have to go back to my homeland. I'm upset because the pepale lookt at me because I have an eye infeson [infection]." Xee, the mother who returned to her homeland with her child Denise, recorded in her journal:

> I feel sad but the child is important to me. I rether go back because I don't know the English. [I will] save some money for some food, for my children can go to school, and buy a house. I was scared because my children where sick, because I'll miss my husband.

We closed the simulation with a large group discussion to encourage students to make explicit what they learned and clarify their questions or misconceptions. Students shared their speculations about how immigrants might have felt about entering the United States through Ellis Island, the different experiences their family had while passing through this entry point, and summaries of what they learned overall about Ellis Island through the simulation.

During individual interviews at the end of the unit, most students could describe at least one main procedure immigrants went through at Ellis Island. Many remembered the health inspections that might lead to immigrants having to return to their homeland if they had diseases. Jacob empathized with new immigrants, but also understood why those with illnesses were returned to their homeland:

> I wouldn't like it because if you had an illness you would get stamped and you had chalk on you. I think the immigrants felt worse because we didn't have chalk written on us and people didn't laugh at us because they could hardly see if we had an illness. But we really didn't. The ones with illness, they didn't want the people in America to get another sickness, so they sent the people with the illness back.[37]

A few students recalled the difficult decisions family members had to make if part of the family had a disease while the rest of the family was healthy. They had to decide whether to return to their homeland with their ill family member or stay in the United States. For example, Hua explained why not all could enter the United States even after a long journey from their homeland:

> I learned that some people could come and had to go back to their homeland, some had rashes or some were getting sick or some had eye infections. They probably felt sad. My family had to stay back. I felt sad because we've come a long way and they tell us to go back.[38]

A few were also impressed with the many questions immigrants were asked and the chalk marks made on immigrants' clothing to identify diseases or other health problems they had. Mandy was especially articulate about the confusion many non-English speaking immigrants might have experienced at Ellis Island.

> [They probably felt] really confused and uncomfortable because they were putting marks on their clothes and they were probably like, "Well, why are they doing this to me? This is probably a bad thing." They looked at the people next to them and wondered, "Who are they?" They probably felt lost and they didn't know where to go and they didn't know the language. There was all these people. Well, I'll just put it this way, they probably felt like people were trying to be mean to them because of the marks and because they were talking to them and it sounds like just a bunch of noises to them because they didn't know the language. They were like, "Why are these people making these noises at me?"when they were trying to talk to them and stuff. They didn't understand.[39]

FOCUS ON YOUR STATE: STUDYING IMMIGRATION EXPERIENCES

Once you know the main cultural groups in your state, you might explore different resources to address the experiences of people who immigrated to your state.

• Contact the tribal offices and reservations of Native American nations living in your state to discover if the nations voluntarily moved or were forced to relocate to your state. Invite an elder or other tribal member to speak to your class about the experiences of moving to your state.

• For cultural groups who immigrated to your state from different countries, investigate their point of entry to the United States, such as Ellis Island and Angel Island. Request additional background information on the immigrants' experience of passing through these points of entry. As a starting point, review the article "The Immigration Stations" in the January, 1983, issue of *Cobblestone* for some background information.[40] Several issues of *Cobblestone*, a U.S. history magazine for children, focus on the theme of immigration and different immigrant groups in the United States, including Japanese Americans, Greek Americans, and Hispanic Americans.

• Use or modify the "Gateway" Ellis Island simulation available from Interact or an online simulation, "The Virtual Ellis Island Tour," which portrays four characters leaving their homelands of Greece, Germany, Poland, and Spain in the early twentieth century, traveling in steerage, and entering the United States through Ellis Island. At Ellis Island the characters must travel through the waiting room, the initial document station, the personal document station, the education and occupation station, the character station, the communication station, the health station, and the physical abilities station. The tour is available at *www.capital.net/~alta/index.html*.

EXPLORING EARLY IMMIGRANTS' EVERYDAY LIFE: STANDARDS AND RECOMMENDED PRACTICES

For the final component of this state history unit, we wanted students to understand different aspects of everyday life among immigrants to our state during the late nineteenth and early twentieth centuries. A history workshop approach[41] allowed us to address some of the standards and recommended social studies practices. When elementary students participate in a history workshop, they use primary sources, such as photographs and artifacts, and read history stories to help them construct an understanding of times past. The class read a trade book describing how one immigrant family met their basic needs during this period. To help students understand aspects of everyday life, the students investigated photographs and artifacts dealing with building homes, growing and preparing food, and making and washing clothes. As students worked in small groups to discuss interpretations of the photographs, artifacts, and the trade book, they were involved in working with others to construct knowledge, an important component of social constructivism.[42] Inquiry into the use of artifacts is also one of the best teaching practices for social studies.[43]

By reading and analyzing *Little House in the Big Woods*[44] as a class, we hoped students would learn about aspects of everyday life for immigrants to Wisconsin, such as the Ingalls family, who lived in an isolated area of the state in the 1870s. Although we were aware of criticisms of this text, including the somewhat romanticized depiction of the Ingalls' family life and the racist characterizations of Native people in several *Little House* books, we could identify no other text that was appropriate for fourth grade students that was still in print. We would have preferred a text that made the cultural background of the immigrant family more explicit, such as the Polish culture portrayed in *First Farm in the Valley: Anna's Story*,[45] but discovered this text was no longer in print.[46] In contrast, *Little House in the Big Woods* provides very little information regarding the Ingalls family's cultural background. However, we used the text to help students understand that newcomers to our state had to produce much of their basic necessities with limited tools, making these tasks very time consuming. In addition, we encouraged students to understand that immigrant families helped each other and had time for recreation, too.

We continued to emphasize the national social studies thematic strand of Time, Continuity, and Change by exploring how European immigrants lived in our state during the late nineteenth century, and we emphasized the People, Places, and Environments thematic strand by investigating how early immigrants' lifestyles were affected by their physical environment.[47] Literacy was an important component of our state history curriculum, and we addressed several of the school district's literacy objectives. We provided the fourth graders with opportunities to:

• Use a variety of comprehension strategies to gain meaning from more complex text.

• Summarize the main topic, main ideas, and supporting details of a text.

• Respond to a text in writing in order to show the meanings inferred from a text.

• Analyze text for the author's purpose and understand character traits and actions.

• Evaluate the behavior of characters from different cultural perspectives.

Integrating a Trade Book with State History: A History Workshop Approach

In our introduction to *Little House in the Big Woods*, a text we read throughout the four weeks of the curriculum unit, we encouraged the students to speculate on reasons for reading this text while we studied Wisconsin history, identified the setting for the story on a state map, and questioned when the author wrote the text. As a way of addressing potential biases and inaccuracies in the author's perspective on events, an important aspect of critical literacy,[48] we also asked students to consider how the author's descriptions of her family life might be affected by the sixty-year time span between when the events occurred and when she wrote the text. Although no student questioned why Pa told Laura and Mary the story of when he was a young boy pretending to "stalk" Indians and fight Indians "until the woods was full of wild men" (p. 54), we wanted to bring out in class discussions the author's European American perspective and bias in this depiction of Native people. One student said it was brave to "fight Indians" while another recognized that immigrants and Native people fought over land. When the author said Ma made "rye'n'Injun" bread for Christmas (p. 62), we asked what kind of bread this was and referred students to *The Little House Cookbook: Frontier Foods from Laura Ingalls Wilder's Classic Stories*[49] for more information. We also asked how Native people might feel about the term "Injun."

We were careful to analyze the book with students to explore the roles of different family members; appropriate behavior for adults and children during this era; how the family produced their food, clothing, and shelter; and various forms of transportation used by immigrants. We emphasized the importance of both Ma's and Pa's contributions to the family with nearly all the food preparation and clothing construction being done by Ma. Students were encouraged to compare their own family activities to those described in the text. Because Hmong families were often farmers in Laos prior to the Vietnam War, we asked the Hmong fourth graders to notice similarities and differences in farming in the state and their homeland.

In their journals, students created character webs showing Ma's, Pa's, Mary's and Laura's important character traits and webs showing the different ways immigrants like the Wilder family obtained their food and had fun. Students also recorded summaries of main ideas learned from their reading, prevalent activities during each season, and responses to such open-ended questions as: What were Sundays like for immigrants? How did immigrants like Ma and Pa deal with bears they encountered? Additionally, students prepared drawings illustrating their conceptions of the setting for the text. In order to help all students construct meaning, we used such strategies as reading aloud to the class, asking students to read with a partner, or allowing students to choose to read alone, with a teacher, or with an audiotaped recording of the text.

During individual interviews at the close of the unit, most students could generalize that life as an immigrant was "hard" due to the necessity of making most of what families needed without modern tools and conveniences. As Charlotte explained, immigrants couldn't purchase many necessities:

> If they wanted anything, they practically had to do it themselves, because, like if they wanted clothes made, they had to do it themselves. If they wanted presents made, they had to do it themselves. They sometimes went to the store to get a little bit of sugar, but very rarely.[50]

Everyone learned that immigrants living in the state during the 1870s, such as Laura Ingalls Wilder's family, had to produce most of their own food. A few recognized their survival depended on obtaining this necessity: "They had to work very hard to survive in the winter. If they didn't work hard, they wouldn't have very much food for the girls to eat."[51] Students recognized that European immigrants obtained food through hunting; growing gardens; killing farm animals such as pigs and smoking or salting the meat; milking cows and making their own butter and cheese; gathering maple sap and making maple sugar; and baking their own bread.

Most of the fourth graders understood that immigrants living in Wisconsin during the late nineteenth century had to make their own clothes. They could purchase fabric at a store some distance from their home, but then they must sew the clothes from this fabric. Many students explained that usually women sewed the clothes, but a few recognized this gendered division of labor was not always so distinct.

> They had to go to town and traded for cloth and stuff. Ma sewed a lot of dresses for Laura and Mary, the good dresses they wore to town. Ma learned how to sew really good. Pa sometimes sewed. He sewed an apron or something for Ma.[52]

All students learned that immigrant children living in our state during the late nineteenth century had simple avenues for enjoying themselves as well as working hard. They played in the snow; played with simple objects such as homemade dolls, stored vegetables, and a pig's bladder; swung from the tree swing; climbed trees; listened to stories; and visited with others. Some recognized the limited places children could play during this period.

> They played outside and they played with the toy dolls that they made. They played in the attic. They would play in their tree house and sung stuff or with fake people that were made out of wood [whittled dolls Pa carved].[53]

Most students identified immigrant adults' recreational activities during the late nineteenth century as playing the fiddle, singing songs, dancing at family dances, telling stories, playing with their children, and visiting with others. In addition, Danny speculated that some of the other activities Pa did were enjoyable:

> He might have had fun killing bears for food. He would make little wooden dolls for Laura and Mary, like the two, I think there is two of them, that they have in the doll houses. He fiddled for them in the winter. For example, at Uncle George's party, he fiddled there and sang and stuff.[54]

Inquiring with Artifacts and Photographs: A History Workshop Approach

Late nineteenth and early twentieth century food and clothing preparation artifacts were employed to encourage students to investigate tangible objects and speculate about what they were and how they were used. See Figure 2–6. We believed if students handled concrete objects similar to those used by early immigrants, the fourth graders would understand more about the everyday lives of Wisconsin immigrants a century ago. These artifacts were obtained from a former teacher education student who had an antique business. Although we expressed our desire for artifacts dealing with food and clothing preparation during the late nineteenth century to correspond closely to the tools described in *Little House in the Big Woods*, these artifacts were not always available.

Once we had the artifacts, we prepared four stations around the classroom for students to work in small groups to investigate their artifacts cooperatively. At one station, students explored the food preparation artifacts of a glass butter churn, butter paddle, and butter mold. At another, they investigated a chocolate stir [metal baton-shaped utensil used in candy making] and brass candy kettle. At a third station, students analyzed a copper measuring pitcher and large iron dipper, while at a fourth, they explored a pig scraper and berry

FIGURE 2–6 Students explore the butter making artifacts

scoop. At the last station, students investigated the clothing preparation artifact of a large yarn winder. At each station, students cooperatively discussed these questions: What do you think these artifacts are?
What were they used for? How do you think they were used? What
materials were they made from? What do these artifacts tell you about
what life was like for immigrants to our state? After they shared their
ideas in the small group, each student recorded responses to the questions, taking into account the ideas of others in the group. At the close
of these small group investigations, students shared what they learned
about the artifacts in a large class discussion. We encouraged students
to elaborate on what led them to conclude what each object was and
its purpose, then we corrected or affirmed their conclusions. Sometimes we discovered the students preferred their own artifact def-
initions to ours! Several students thought the pig scraper, used to
scrape the bristles off a pig after it was killed and scalded for butcher-
ing, was a nut cracker. They demonstrated how immigrants could
place an unshelled nut on a table and use the flat side of the pig scraper
to hit it hard, which broke the shell and made the nut ready for eating.

During the interviews, most students demonstrated learning
from the artifact activity. A number of the fourth graders explained
the challenge of identifying what the artifacts were because many are
no longer used. John said it succinctly, "They were hard to guess because they were back then and we have better stuff these days."[55]

> First on station four, at first we thought it was a big comb, it looked
> like a comb, so we thought it was a horse's brush. There was another
> one that we thought was a nutcracker. You go like this (pounded his
> fists against each other), there was a screw on the bottom, when you
> hit the nut, it would break. [That was] for a pig, it would take its skin
> off with the sharp ends on the circle part. [The other] was for digging
> up the roots or the weeds or stuff like that in the garden.[56]

It was more challenging for students to generalize that these artifacts
reflected the challenges of producing food and clothing for early state
immigrants, but a few did. "It was hard, very hard. It was like, all day
churning and churning. You work so hard and you hardly get anything."[57] Only one student explained the value of the artifacts in understanding tools immigrants used.

Those activities really helped me to understand things better so that I know what they used and what they really looked like, not just by looking at pictures because sometimes pictures don't give the real details about it. The kettle, the mixer, they sort of go together because you could carry water or cook [with them]. Maple sugar was in it. You could carry it in the bucket. I didn't know it was like that. I thought it was wooden and that really helped me understand that better.[58]

In addition to analyzing artifacts, students worked in small groups to investigate copies of photographs published by the State Historical Society that portrayed various aspects of the lives of immigrants to Wisconsin.[59] One group inquired into photographs of an immigrant wagon train and African American settlement in one area of the state; another group focused on photographs of log cabin homes; a third group studied photographs of men working together to build homes and barns; a fourth group investigated photographs of women churning butter and the storage of cream and butter in a spring house; a fifth group analyzed photographs of a kitchen with a sink, stove, and assorted kitchen tools as well as a woman washing clothes in a tub outside; and the last group examined photographs of spinning, weaving, and sewing cloth. As the students worked in small groups, they discussed and recorded their ideas to these questions: Who is in each picture? What objects do you see in the picture? What seems to be happening in each picture? What does each picture tell you about what life was like for state immigrants? What might it be like to live during this time? Finally, each small group shared their photographs and analyses with the rest of the class, especially what the photographs illustrated about immigrant life. We expanded on their interpretations with additional background information on the objects, activities, and settings for the photographs.

When Charlotte, John, and Kay described their interpretation of the picture of African Americans in front of a building, they decided because everyone was holding lunch pails and books, they were standing in front of a school or home. They concluded life for immigrants was hard because "they didn't have much stuff and they had a lot of kids." We elaborated that the picture of African Americans illustrated that people from similar backgrounds often lived together once they moved to the state.

Patty, Susan, and Neal speculated their picture of a log cabin home belonged to Laura's aunt and uncle (from *Little House in the Big Woods*) and the pig pen beside the home would keep the pig from running around in the woods and getting a disease. These fourth graders also surmised that immigrant life was difficult because "they had to cut down wood to build houses." We encouraged the students to think about how warm the log cabins were and the amount of space children had for playing inside.

During the interviews, half of the fourth graders described something they learned from analyzing pictures of everyday life for immigrants in the state during the nineteenth century. They spoke of understanding early schools; the different clothing styles and machines used during the period; and the difficulties of building homes and other structures, making clothes, weaving cloth, pumping water, and doing laundry.

> My picture was a person doing the wash in the kitchen with tons of stuff. I learned it was hard for the lady to do their own laundry. The kitchen is so small. The sink was bigger than ours and different. It kind of looked like a tub for a baby.[60]

FOCUS ON YOUR STATE: INVESTIGATING THE LIFESTYLE OF YOUR STATE'S IMMIGRANTS THROUGH A HISTORY WORKSHOP

In order to encourage your students to understand life during earlier times among immigrants to your state, you might explore different sources for trade books, artifacts, and photographs.

• Contact your local library, bookstore, historical society, and Native American tribal offices or museums for names of children's trade books portraying the lifestyle of diverse immigrants at different periods in your state's history.

• Once you have identified trade books to use, look for artifacts and photographs corresponding to the time period and immigrant groups portrayed in the trade books. Check with local antique shops, museums, historians, the local or state historical society, and Native American tribal offices and museums for artifacts and photographs. Your local library may also have old photographs of life in your community and state during earlier times.

After collecting all the materials for the history workshop, you might:

• Create learning centers or other small group activities to allow your students ample opportunities to examine and discuss the photographs and artifacts.

• Provide plenty of discussion time for your students to explain their interpretations of the photographs and artifacts and what led them to their conclusions.

• Using the trade book you read as a class, guide your students in making connections between the photographs and artifacts.

• Assist your students in making generalizations about what the lives of early immigrants were like based on their interpretations of the artifacts, photographs, and trade books.

REFLECTIONS AND RECOMMENDATIONS

We were delighted with the balance we achieved in addressing multicultural ideas and national, state, and local school district standards in part of the first state history unit. Both components were integrated well within our focus on the different cultural groups who became part of the state and the connection between students' family histories and state history. The fourth graders were excited to share their family histories with the rest of the class. This increased their understanding of their own family history and at least one distinct cultural group who immigrated to Wisconsin. Our experiences affirmed our belief that when history is made personal for elementary students, they are much more interested and engaged and will likely learn. We encourage you to look for the state standards you will meet when you focus on the cultural diversity among your students' families. By beginning with family history, your students are more likely to be drawn into your state history curriculum.

We continue to address the multicultural focus of the unit through a stronger emphasis on Native nations as the first people to live in our state. One simple method of integrating Native Americans is through family history. If your students' cultural backgrounds include Native American ancestry, Native people's origins in the state could be integrated through family history as well as through the research of the main cultural groups that constitute the state's population.

We continue to search for additional resources, including original documents accessible for students to read and understand, as they research why distinct cultural groups left their homelands and settled in the state. Original documents often reflect immigrants' firsthand experiences for students to interpret rather than sort through the biases and perspectives of the authors of secondary sources. Focusing on the experiences of immigrants from different parts of the world and from different times, and their lifestyle once they settled in the state can also enrich the multicultural content. Students especially benefit from hearing directly from additional guest speakers, such as Rameen's mother, who recently immigrated to the state. Guest speakers can describe the benefits and challenges of leaving their homeland, entering the United States, and arriving in the state. We encourage you to consult with your local and state historical societies, museums, and libraries for original documents portraying immigrants' experiences. Also contact local human service organizations who assist recent refugees and immigrants for possible guest speakers.

We were also pleased with the students' interest, engagement, and learning from the history workshop approach[61] and its compatibility with social constructivist teaching methods[62] and best teaching practices in social studies.[63] Such diverse activities appealed to most of our students and should enrich your own state history curriculum. Further refinements of our experiences with this approach include finding trade books that portray specific cultural backgrounds of immigrants in Wisconsin to illustrate the influence of their homeland culture on their new lifestyle in a different country. We continue to search for photographs and artifacts that more closely correspond to those used in the trade book we read as a class. The characters in the text *Little House in the Big Woods*[64] use a wooden butter churn rather than the later glass model we investigated in our artifact activity. By providing more representative artifacts, students could use the text as a context for investigating the objects, draw on the understandings they gained from the text as they analyzed the artifacts, and use the artifacts to enrich the meanings they gain from the text. By working with local and state historical societies, museums, antique shops, Native American tribal offices, and bookstores, you are more likely to identify appropriate trade books, artifacts, and photographs of times past.

ENDNOTES

1. Interview with Mandy, 9/25/97; all students' names are pseudonyms.
2. A number of Hmong people prefer the Hmong identification rather than Hmong American.
3. National Council for the Social Studies, *Expectations of Excellence: Curriculum Standards for Social Studies* (Washington, DC: National Council for the Social Studies, 1994), 49–50.
4. Hal Balsiger, Paula DeHart, Margaret A. Laughlin, Stephen A. Rose, and Michael Yell, *Planning Curriculum in Social Studies* (Madison, WI: Wisconsin Department of Public Instruction, 2001), 117.
5. Balsiger et al., 40.
6. Ibid.
7. Christine A. Sleeter and Carl A. Grant, *Making Choices for Multicultural Education: Five Approaches to Race, Class, and Gender,* 3rd ed. (Upper Saddle River, NJ: Merrill,1999), 188–216.
8. Donna C. Creighton, "Critical Literacy in the Elementary Classroom," *Language Arts* 74 (1997), 438–445; Carole Edelsky, "Education for Democracy," in JoBeth Allen, ed., *Class Actions: Teaching for Social Justice in Elementary and Middle School* (New York: Teachers College Press,1999), 147–156; Carole Edelsky, "On Critical Whole Language Practice: Why, What, and a Bit of How," in Carole Edelsky, ed., *Making Justice Our Project: Teachers Working Toward Critical Whole Language Practice* (Urbana, IL: National Council of Teachers of English, 1999), 19–36.
9. Betsy Maestro, *Coming to America: The Story of Immigration* (New York: Scholastic, 1996).

10. Steven Zemelman, Harvey Daniels, and Arthur Hyde, *Best Practice: New Standards for Teaching and Learning in America's Schools* (Portsmouth, NH: Heinemann, 1998), 132–155.

11. Carrie Rothstein-Fisch, Patricia M. Greenfield, and Elise Trumball, "Bridging Cultures with Classroom Strategies," *Educational Leadership* 56 (1999), 64–67. We recognize not all Mexican American and Hmong students prefer cooperative learning activities and not all European American students value individual learning activities. Historically, individual learning opportunities have been emphasized in schools over cooperative learning, which led to educational advantages for students from cultural backgrounds embracing individualism.

12. Delores Johnson, *Now Let Me Fly: The Story of a Slave Family* (New York: Macmillan, 1993).

13. Jacob Lawrence, *The Great Migration: An American Story* (New York: HarperCollins, 1993).

14. Dia Cha, *Dia's Story Cloth* (New York: Lee & Low, 1996).

15. Interview with Jake, 9/24/97.

16. Interview with Charlotte, 9/25/97.

17. Interview with Mandy, 9/25/97.

18. Interview with Carlos, 9/24/97.

19. Cha.

20. Interview with Tong, 9/25/97.

21. Sleeter and Grant, 189.

22. Zemelman et al., 155.

23. Balsiger et al., 61–62.

24. Interview with Carlos, 9/24/97.

25. Interview with Jake, 9/24/97.

26. Ibid.

27. Interview with Charlotte, 9/25/97.

28. Judy's K-W-L chart, 9/24/97, on which Judy lists what she *knows* about the topic, what she *wants* to know, and what she *learned*.

29. Interview with Mandy, 9/25/97.

30. Ira Wolfman, *Do People Grow on Family Trees? Genealogy for Kids & Other Beginners* (New York: Workman Publishing, 1991); Maureen Taylor, *Through the Eyes of Your Ancestors: A Step-by-Step Guide to Uncovering Your Family's History* (Boston: Houghton Mifflin Company, 1999).

31. National Council for the Social Studies, 51.

32. Balsiger et al., 61.

33. Jere Brophy and Janet Alleman, *Powerful Social Studies for Elementary Students* (New York: Harcourt Brace, 1996), 63–77; Geoffrey

Scheurman, "From Behaviorist to Constructivist Teaching," *Social Education* 62 (1998), 6–9.

34. Zemelman et al., 155.
35. Jay Mack, Paul DeKock, and Dave Yount, *Gateway: A Simulation of Immigration Issues in Past and Present America* (Carlsbad, CA: Interact, 1993), 1–7.
36. Steven Kroll, *Ellis Island: Doorway to Freedom* (New York: Holiday House, 1995); Ellen Levine, *If Your Name Was Changed at Ellis Island* (New York: Scholastic, 1993).
37. Interview with Jacob, 9/25/97.
38. Interview with Hua, 9/25/97.
39. Interview with Mandy, 9/25/97.
40. Donald Lankiewicz, "The Immigration Stations," *Cobblestone* 4 (1983), 6–9.
41. Karen L. Jorgensen, *History Workshop: Reconstructing the Past with Elementary Students* (Portsmouth, NH: Heinemann, 1993), 13–25.
42. Brophy and Alleman, 63–77; Scheurman, 6–9.
43. Zemelman et al., 155.
44. Laura Ingalls Wilder, *Little House in the Big Woods* (New York: HarperTrophy, 1971).
45. Anne Pellowski, *First Farm in the Valley: Anna's Story* (Winona, MN: Saint Mary's Press, 1982).
46. *First Farm in the Valley: Anna's Story* was originally published by Putnam Publishing Group, but went out of print. We later discovered *First Farm in the Valley: Anna's Story* and other books in the series about this Polish family were republished by Saint Mary's Press and are still in print.
47. National Council for the Social Studies, 51, 54.
48. Creighton, 438–445; Edelsky, "Education for Democracy," 147–156.
49. Barbara M. Walker, *The Little House Cookbook: Frontier Foods From Laura Ingalls Wilder's Classic Stories* (New York: HarperTrophy, 1979), 86–87.
50. Interview with Charlotte, 9/25/97.
51. Interview with Susan, 9/24/97.
52. Interview with Danny, 9/24/97.
53. Interview with John, 9/25/97.
54. Interview with Danny, 9/24/97.
55. Interview with John, 9/25/97.
56. Interview with Rameen, 9/24/97.
57. Interview with Patty, 9/24/97.

58. Interview with Susan, 9/24/97.
59. Artifacts and photographs might be available from local and state historical societies, local and state museums, local libraries, and private collections.
60. Interview with Chia, 9/25/97.
61. Jorgensen, 13–25.
62. Brophy and Alleman, 63–77; Scheurman, 6–9.
63. Zemelman et al., 155.
64. Wilder.

CHAPTER 3

LEARNING ABOUT THE FIRST PEOPLE
IN THE STATE: TRADITIONS
AND CONFLICTS

Danny, Judy, John, Denise, and Maria stood in the front of the classroom dramatizing the treaty negotiations between the U.S. government and the Ho-Chunk, one of the six federally recognized Native nations in our state. Before the students presented their dramatization, they read and discussed a reading from *Visions and Voices: Winnebago Elders Speak to the Children*,[1] which gave a Ho-Chunk perspective on their loss of land through treaties with the U.S. government. With our guidance, the four students planned and presented their dramatization of the main events in the reading.

John (Ho-Chunk narrator): It is 1829. Our people were persuaded to give up more than two million acres and paid $18,000.

Danny (U.S. governmental official, speaking to the four Ho-Chunk): We want two million acres of land.

Judy (Ho-Chunk): What will you give us?

Danny: We'll give you $18,000 a year for thirty years.

Judy: We'll have to think about it.

(Judy and the other Ho-Chunk whisper among themselves.)

Judy: We'll give up land.

John: A few years passed. It's 1832, they started after more land.

Danny: We want two million acres of land.

Judy: What will you give us?

Danny: $10,000 for the next thirty years and a school.

John (Ho-Chunk child): Do I have to go to school?

74

Denise (John's Ho-Chunk mother): I don't want you to lose your Indian ways.

Judy: We still won't give up our land.

Danny: You have to give up your land. You have to leave your land.

(Judy, Denise, and Maria all sign a piece of paper which Danny placed on the table.)

Danny (holds up the signed paper): Eight months to get off the land.

Judy: First you said eight years, now you say eight months. It's just not fair!

Danny: You have to leave now.

Maria (Ho-Chunk): Maybe we'll share the land with you.

Another group of students dramatized the treaty negotiations between the Menominee and the U.S. government with some assistance from us. To prepare for their presentation, they read "Oshkosh and Menominee Lands" from *Badger History* magazine,[2] written from a European American perspective with some empathy for the Menominee experiences.

Jake (Governor Dodge, approaches three Menominee tribal members): We would like to buy some land from you.

Xee (Menominee): We have to think about it. What will you give us?

Jake: $700,000 for forty million acres.

Xee: We'll think about it (discusses the message with Chia and Tong, other Menominee).

(The Menominee consent to sell the land and Governor Dodge gives them "money" for land.)

Xee: That's only seventeen cents an acre. That's not fair for us!

Kay and Hua (U.S. governmental officials speaking to three Menominee): We want all your land. If you give us all your land, you can move to Minnesota.

Xee: We'll make the trip to Minnesota.

(The Menominee walk around the front of the classroom to illustrate the journey to Minnesota, stop, and look around.)

Chia (Menominee): There's no animals.

Xee (Menominee): There's no food.

Tong (Menominee Chief Oshkosh): No wild rice.

Xee: What can we do here? Nothing to hunt!

Chia: What will we take?

(Menominee walks around the front of the classroom to illustrate the return to Wisconsin.)

Xee (with other Menominee speaking to President Fillmore): President Fillmore, the government wants us to go to Minnesota, but there's no food.

Chia (to President Fillmore): No animals.

Tong (to President Fillmore): No wild rice.

Xee: So what should we do here?

Patty (President Fillmore): I'll fill out a piece of paper and you can stay there [Wisconsin] for years.

In the follow-up class discussion, we asked the students if the treaty negotiations were fair for the U.S. government and Native people. Two students suggested, "The government got something out of it, but the Indians didn't," and "The U.S. government was getting all the land, that's what they wanted, but the Indians were being forced off the land." This scene from the second unit, which lasted two months, illustrated our efforts to help students learn about the six federally recognized Native nations of Wisconsin, including the Ho-Chunk, Menominee, Ojibwa, Potawatomi, the Stockbridge-Munsee band of Mohicans, and the Oneida. The unit had the strongest multicultural content of our state history curriculum and the greatest emphasis on critical literacy. We hoped the fourth graders would understand Native people's cultural values regarding land and their perspectives about interactions with the U.S. government. Students had many opportunities to walk in the shoes of Native Americans as we investigated Native people's traditional lifestyle before contact with Europeans, changes precipitated by the fur trade and continued contact with European Americans, and conflicts with the U.S. government over treaties, movement to reservations, and children's forced attendance at boarding schools. The fourth graders not only learned, but empathized with and became indignant about some of the injustices experienced by Native people in Wisconsin.

NATIVE AMERICAN CULTURAL VALUES AND TRADITIONAL LIFESTYLE

We introduced the unit with a focus on the cultural values and traditional lifestyle of the Ho-Chunk, Menominee, Ojibwa, Potawatomi, Oneida, and the Stockbridge-Munsee band of Mohicans prior to contact with Europeans. Students completed research, illustrated their findings, read, discussed, and responded to trade books as they constructed understandings of the cultures and cultural diversity among Wisconsin Native people.

School District, State, and National Standards

The Culture thematic strand[3] was a strong element of the unit, addressing both an important national standard and significant multicultural theme. We wanted the fourth graders to understand the values, beliefs, and lifestyle of the six Native nations in the state including the importance of group identity, generosity, contributions to the group's well-being, and respect for the natural world to help each nation survive. The Culture thematic strand also addressed a specific Behavioral Sciences state and local social studies standard:

• Students will investigate and explain similarities and differences in ways that cultures meet human needs.[4]

Native people's respect for their physical environment, shown by adapting to it and taking only what was needed, was an important cultural value and part of the national People, Places and Environments thematic strand.[5] Students learned not only where each nation lived originally, but how the physical environment influenced the six nation's traditional lifestyles and how they met their basic needs for food, clothing, and shelter. The state and local standards in Geography: People, Places, and Environments were similar.

• Students will describe and give examples of ways in which people interact with the physical environment, including use of land, location of communities, methods of construction, and design of shelters.[6]

Multicultural Ideas, Critical Literacy, and Literacy

Similar to the Culture thematic strand is the multicultural theme of incorporating the experiences and perspectives of diverse groups of people, such as the six Native American nations in the state.[7] We introduced the Native nations' traditional lifestyles and the roles of women, men, elders, and children through small group research using carefully selected print resources. The fourth graders also read and discussed various trade books portraying Native people's food gathering and growing and powwow traditions and the cultural beliefs and values which provided the foundation for these traditions.

We addressed several school district literacy objectives within the social studies unit on Native Americans:

• Use the index, table of contents, and glossary to gain information when reading expository text.

• Use a variety of comprehension strategies to gain meaning from complex text.

• Respond to reading through: role playing, writing logs, or journals; writing responses illustrating inferred meaning; explaining the author's purpose, character traits, and actions from different cultural perspectives; and summarizing expository text with main topic, main ideas, and supporting details.

Critical literacy was incorporated through the selection of texts which provided Native American perspectives on values, beliefs, and traditions. We encouraged students to share and defend their interpretations of the texts and analyze the trade books for point of view, accuracy, and bias. Students investigated who the authors were and speculated as to the author's purpose in writing the text. We elaborated on the authors' credibility for writing an authentic text about indigenous people. As small groups read different texts, they summarized important ideas in whole class discussions, compared and contrasted the texts, and checked for point of view, accuracy, and bias in all texts. The fourth graders were asked to compare themselves to the main characters of the texts and question their interpretations.

BEST TEACHING PRACTICES AND CULTURALLY RELEVANT, SOCIAL CONSTRUCTIVIST METHODS

Small Group Research

In order to encourage students to work together cooperatively in constructing knowledge of the six federally recognized Native American nations in Wisconsin, we organized students into small, heterogeneous, cooperative groups.[8] This activity followed two best teaching practices for social studies:

• Explore a variety of cultures.

• Form mixed ability groups and have students participate in interactive and cooperative study processes.[9]

In addition, we continued to implement different aspects of culturally relevant teaching.[10] We emphasized the traditional Hmong and Mexican American cultural value of cooperation[11] to support students' learning from these cultural backgrounds. As students worked in small, cooperative groups, we, along with Kristen, our research assistant, monitored the groups very carefully to make sure each student was involved and contributed to the activity. We invited participation from quiet group members and encouraged vocal students to solicit contributions from less assertive fourth graders. During large group follow-up discussions, we asked students who tended to remain silent, mostly Hmong students and a few girls from European American and Mexican American backgrounds, to report the results of their group work for the class.

Each small group first selected one of the Wisconsin Native nations to study by drawing the name of one of the nations out of a basket. Then, with our guidance, the group of three or four students researched the food, clothing, and shelter that the Native people created from their physical environment and the roles of women, men, elders, and children in meeting basic necessities before European contact. Students read texts and studied illustrations and photographs during their research, as shown in Figure 3–1.[12] One or two group members read aloud important ideas from the texts while one or two of the remaining group members took notes on these ideas. Their final product was a visual representation of what they learned from their investigation. For example, Xee, Jacob, and Patty examined the Menominee and created a chart showing two styles of houses, one for warm weather and another for cold weather. They wrote, "The Menominee people either caught or planted their food. They flavored food with berries and maple syrup. Wild rice was gathered in the fall. They decorated clothes with porcupine quills and shells."

After each group finished their chart, they placed them on tables in the classroom. The class did a "silent share," in which all students

FIGURE 3–1 Students cooperatively research Native people's traditional lifestyles before European contact

silently walked around the classroom carefully observing each group's chart and mentally checking for similarities and differences in each nation's food, clothing, and shelter. In the follow-up class discussion, students listed similarities and we recorded them on the board:

They all lived in wooded areas.

Houses came from wood.

They hunted, gathered, or grew food.

Their clothing came from animals.

In interviews at the end of the unit, nearly all students could accurately describe the food, clothing, and shelter of Native people from the state.

Research groups created another chart illustrating at least one important role for women, men, elders, and children. Charts depicted women taking care of children, gardening, picking berries, cooking food, and making pots, baskets, and clothing. Groups also illustrated men hunting and fishing for food, harvesting wild rice, making bows and arrows, and helping build dwellings on charts. Students learned these roles were crucial for keeping children alive and providing the food and clothing everyone needed to live. Elders' roles were portrayed as caring for and teaching children and passing on stories. These activities were important for continuing traditions and stories so they would not be forgotten. The children's roles included helping and learning from their parents and playing with materials in their environment (such as deer sticks). It was important for the children to assist their parents in providing food for the nation and to learn what they needed to know as adults. During the end-of-unit interviews, nearly all students explained at least one role filled by women, men, children, and elders and the majority elaborated on their importance. Mandy knew the significance of play for children and storytelling for elders:

> If they [children] didn't learn how to play with the stuff that was around them, then they wouldn't learn how to use the stuff when they needed things when they grew up. [Elders] told stories to young children so they could pass on the stories of the tradition. It was

traditional. If they didn't pass on the stories, they would lose the tradition.[13]

Charlotte understood the importance of each person's contributions to the Native nation: "If everyone does their job, the whole thing combines and then it is all done. Everybody takes a part."[14] Denise clarified the importance of everyone working together to meet the people's basic needs:

> The elders' job was pretty important because the women and men were pretty busy, so teaching the children was an important thing because nobody else really had time to do it. The children's job, playing, is kind of important because they are not in the way of any hunting or doing important things. The women's jobs were important because they take care of the food source and the clothing. The men's jobs was pretty much to do the basic foods like meat and the fish. The women had to garden. You can't live without vegetables, so they gardened. So everything was real important.[15]

Literature Circles

Critical literacy was integrated with literature circles as we read and discussed three well-illustrated trade books dealing with Native people's traditional food gathering or growing traditions as they continue today among the Ojibwa and Ho-Chunk and the beliefs which are the foundation for these traditions. Students selected which text they wanted to read, then we created heterogeneous groups of students based on the text they chose, literacy level, gender, and cultural background. Each group decided how they would read the text, either individually, with a partner, or with everyone in the small group. To guide the discussion, we gave students a list of questions about the reading for them to discuss among themselves in their literature circles. We participated in the discussion, but encouraged students to lead the discussion and invite everyone's contributions. Following their group discussion, students recorded a summary of what they learned from the text in their journals. We began each text by investigating the authors' backgrounds and their purpose for writing the text.

The Sacred Harvest[16] focuses on one Ojibwa family harvesting and processing wild rice and portrays the belief that Ojibwa people should put tobacco on the water as an offering for a good harvest. Students learned that wild rice is an important tradition, a sacred food, and that parents usually teach their children how to gather wild rice in order to continue the tradition. The author is a member of the Leech Lake band of Ojibwa in Minnesota, the same reservation portrayed in the text, and harvested wild rice as a young man.

Ininatig's Gift of Sugar[17] depicts an Ojibwa maple sugar camp created for the purpose of teaching the young how to tap maple trees to make maple syrup and sugar. It illustrates some of the steps in the process and clarifies the historical significance of maple sap as providing important food for Ojibwa people during late winter when many of their food supplies were running low. The text emphasizes that families should thank maple trees each spring for their sap and not take this gift for granted. The author is a member of the Seneca nation from New York and has written articles and chapters about Native people.

Four Seasons of Corn[18] portrays a Ho-Chunk family planting, weeding, harvesting, and drying corn for eating. The text describes the entire family's involvement in growing corn and the cultural belief in the importance of giving thanks and tobacco to the Creator for this food. The author is Ojibwa, but is married to a Ho-Chunk, and she and her family have grown and processed corn for twenty years. After reading and discussing the texts in literature circles, students created murals illustrating main ideas, as shown in Figure 3–2.

During individual interviews, most students described what they learned about traditional food gathering and growing among the Ojibwa and Ho-Chunk from reading one of the trade books. During large group discussions, we asked students to summarize important ideas from their text for the rest of the class. We encouraged students to teach one another about the specific text they read. Denise was especially articulate about what she learned from the texts:

> I learned that corn isn't just a thing you can do just one time a year
> and it's done. You have to work on it year round. It's not pretty easy.
> I learned there are many, many different kinds of corn. I didn't know

FIGURE 3–2 One group completes a mural illustrating main ideas from *Four Seasons of Corn* during their literature circle

there was that many kinds of corn. They have fun doing it. You think, aw man, I have to work this hard. But they have fun doing it. They wouldn't just eat it for themselves. They would share it with neighbors. They were pretty generous. All ages would help. The smaller kids would pick the corn off the ground if it fell or something. The bigger kids would hoe and pick higher stalks of corn. The parents would watch the younger kids. Everybody was working at the same time. It got done really fast.

What I learned about *The Sacred Harvest* is that they would share with the whole family. They would teach the younger children. Hey it's your turn and now you have to learn how to go wild ricing. If they say yes, here is how you shake it [wild rice] off. At first it looks like it doesn't get very much off ya know, a little rice. Yeah, there is a lot just from one scrape.

From the sugar group, it's kind of neat that he [Porky, Ojibwa elder who leads the sugar camp] lets everybody else do it. There is like a camp and you learn how to do it and you get to take home your own maple syrup. You never think of a tree like, Yeah, it's a tree.

It gives leaves and flowers and stuff. I mean it can't give food. But the maple trees, they can. You never really think about how much you can get from nature. I've never realized it. You know you think of maple syrup, sure it's good on pancakes, but I mean, it's not so important. I can go without maple syrup. To them it's pretty important because they have been doing it for a long time. It was important to their grandfathers and their fathers. They want to keep it going.[19]

Students also worked in literature circles to read one of three well-illustrated texts about the meanings and importance of powwows to Ojibwa. *Powwow Summer: A Family Celebrates the Circle of Life*[20] portrays an Ojibwa family, the Downwinds, who carry on many Ojibwa traditions. They care for foster children, which reflects the Ojibwa belief that all children and all adults are related. Their participation in many powwows over the summer months illustrates the importance of continuing the tradition of joining with friends and families to celebrate the circle of life. They also sponsor a giveaway, a sign of generosity and thankfulness, to thank friends and family members for supporting their daughter's reign as powwow princess. The author is also Ojibwa and traveled to three powwows with the Downwinds family in preparation for the book.

Shannon: An Ojibway Dancer[21] focuses on Shannon, an Ojibwa living in Minneapolis, who does the beadwork for her own powwow outfits and participates in many powwows as a fancy shawl dancer. It elaborates on different types of powwow dancers and the skill and care needed to create many parts of the powwow outfits. The author is also Ojibwa and is from St. Paul, Minnesota.

Nanabosho Dances[22] describes two children who learn how to make and repair their outfits to dance in powwows. As their grandparents help them make the outfits, they also teach them more about Ojibwa culture through stories, such as the meaning of the hoop dance, the importance of eagle feathers on powwow outfits, and the tradition of offering tobacco before taking plants and animals. The author, an Ojibwa, has written many books about Ojibwa legends.

During student-led literature circle discussions, we asked students to respond to such questions as: What am I learning about Ojibwa people from the book? What might the author be trying to tell the reader in this part of the book? What am I learning about myself while I'm learning about Ojibwa people? Denise, Xee, Judy, Jake, and Tong discussed the last question as they read *Shannon: An Ojibway Dancer*. Xee offered, "Hmong put beads on their clothes like the Indians." Jake suggested, "Americans don't wear traditional clothes unless it's Christmas time and they get dressed up to go out to eat or something." Denise added, "Sometimes grandparents sew, like Shannon's family, her grandma sews her shawl." Although Tong had difficulty articulating his idea, other students encouraged him, and he explained, "Indians wear clothes almost the same as the Hmong. Other people don't wear clothes like Hmong."

When Ava joined the group, she explained her interest in how they were making connections between their own lives and the people in the book. Jake quickly responded, "The Hmong had good ideas, but the Americans don't." Ava clarified, "That's interesting, do you mean the Hmong aren't American? Is that true? Xee's and Tong's heritage is Hmong American, Denise is Russian American, Judy is Dutch American, and you are Polish American." Jake then responded, "Hmong Americans had pretty good ideas, they were saying they had special clothes for the New Year, kind of like in the book, but European Americans don't wear special clothes unless it's Christmas and we get dressed up and go out to dinner." Denise added, "Sometimes a grandmother sews something and helps you sew something like the Indians." Xee clarified the importance of the Hmong New Year, playing with friends, bringing and sharing food, and purchasing things from Hmong stores. Judy explained her family's tradition to ride her uncle's horses every Mother's Day, which was similar to the powwow tradition.

By the end of the unit, most students described main ideas about powwows gained from the texts. Denise summarized what she learned from *Shannon: An Ojibway Dancer*:

> It took a long time to make their outfits. They call the dresses with the little cones their jingle dresses. They used snuff can lids and fold them. When you dance, it makes a little jingle sound. Shawl dancing, you have to move your arms a lot. The older kids help the younger kids learn. It's not something you wait until you get up on stage and say, "Uh oh, I didn't practice for this!" You don't just say, "Oh, I'll get my dress done" and then you only have a week to get this done.

So you have to really keep it up. The thing I thought was weird was that Shannon's grandma said, "Don't forget to put a mistake in there!" It looks pretty perfect to me. They believe there is a soul in the moccasin, a spirit or something. The mistake is like a doorway so the spirit can go in and out. It looks so hard when she was beading away. I thought, I could never do that![23]

FOCUS ON YOUR STATE:
NATIVE AMERICAN CULTURAL VALUES
AND TRADITIONAL LIFESTYLES

To discover which Native nations currently live in your state, see *www.nativeamericanonline.com*. For the names of Native nations which resided in your state during earlier periods, contact your state's historical society. Once you know which Native American nations inhabited your state at any time, you might explore different resources for teaching about each nation's traditional cultural values and lifestyles.

• For Native nations currently living in your state, contact the tribal offices or museums for suggestions of teaching resources, such as guest speakers, field trips, photographs, artifacts, videos, trade books, other print materials, and websites. Tribal elders would especially provide authentic explanations of the nation's traditions, values, and lifestyles before contact with Europeans.

• For suggestions of authentic trade books on different Native nations, see the Oyate organization's website, available at *www.oyate.org* or consult book reviews in *Through Indian Eyes: The Native Experience in Books for Children*.[24] Several publishers also offer series of authentic texts on Native Americans, such as the We Are Still Here series published by Lerner, the Native American series produced by Millbrook Press, and the Indians of North America series published by Chelsea House Publishers.

• For very helpful general guidelines and resources in teaching sensitively about different Native American nations, see *Native Americans*

Today: Resources and Activities for Educators Grades 4-8, Teaching About Native Americans, and *How to Teach About American Indians: A Guide for the School Media Specialist.*[25]

NATIVE AMERICAN PERSPECTIVES ON THE FUR TRADE

Our next focus was to introduce the fourth graders to the experiences and perspectives of the Menominee, Ho-Chunk, Ojibwa, Potawatomi, Oneida, and the Stockbridge-Munsee band of Mohicans regarding the first contact with Europeans and how their lives changed over time because of contact with Europeans. Students continued to work in small, heterogeneous, cooperative groups to consider the harmful and beneficial effects of the fur trade on Native people.

Standards and Multicultural Ideas

In our study of the fur trade, we continued to integrate the Culture thematic strand from the national standards, the corresponding Behavioral Sciences: Individuals, Institutions, and Society state and local standards, and the multicultural emphasis on the integration of diverse people's experiences and perspectives in the curriculum.[26] We wanted to emphasize how cultural differences among the European fur traders and Native people contributed to diverse perspectives on the fur trade. In particular, we provided opportunities for students to:

• Describe how differences in cultures may lead to understanding or misunderstanding among people.[27]

In addition, we addressed history standards through the Time, Continuity and Change national thematic strand.[28] Students worked in small groups to investigate the advantages and disadvantages of participating in the fur trade. They also researched how the fur trade eventually changed the lives of people from the Native nation they were studying. Similar state and local standards were addressed as well as the explicit expectation that students would learn about the Native

American nations in Wisconsin. In particular, we provided opportunities for the fourth graders to:

• Identify and examine various sources of information that are used for constructing an understanding of the past, such as maps, textbooks, photographs, and oral presentations.

• Explain the history, culture, and tribal status of the American Indian tribes and bands in Wisconsin.[29]

Small Group Research and Problem Solving

In order to help students examine the fur trade from Native people's perspectives, students remained in their small, heterogeneous, cooperative groups and discussed the beneficial and harmful effects of the fur trade on the six Wisconsin nations. We created a narrative "Should Your Nation Trade Furs?" which explained French or Dutch fur traders' requests to trade, possible changes in lifestyle if the nations agreed to trade, and listed products traders offered to trade for beaver pelts.[30] The fourth graders considered the conflict between the Native American cultural value of taking only the animals needed for basic necessities and the fur traders' cultural value of trapping many animals for trading and earning a profit. Students also studied photographs and drawings of European trade goods.[31] We asked students to place themselves in the position of people from the Native nation they were studying, discuss how participating in the fur trade might help and hurt their members, and decide if they would trade with European traders. An example of one of our discussion guides is shown in Figure 3–3.

When we discussed each group's decision as a class, the fourth graders had mixed views about their Native nation's participation in the fur trade. The Oneida group decided they would not participate in the fur trade because they could make their own pots and did not want to kill animals just for the fur. The Stockbridge-Munsee group of three did not reach a decision. They were concerned they might not have enough animals for food, but they could get clothes from trade cloth. They recognized guns were more effective than bows and arrows, and they would become more "civilized" from participating

SHOULD YOUR NATION TRADE FURS?

Name _____

Work with the others in your group to read the story and discuss the questions. Make sure each person has a chance to say something about each question. If someone does not offer an idea, ask them what their idea is. After each person explains an idea, then write your ideas after the question.

French or Dutch fur traders ask the members of your nation to hunt animals for their furs. The fur traders want many, many furs. They especially want you to hunt or trap beavers. These furs can be used on clothes in Europe. Many European men want to wear hats made from beaver pelt.

The men of your nation usually hunt only enough animals to make sure everyone in the nation has enough food to eat and clothes to wear. They do not hunt for more animals than they need. If you agree to hunt animals for the fur traders, the men would have to spend much more time hunting and being away from their families and nation. The women would have to spend much more time processing the furs to get them ready to trade. Women would have less time to make baskets or pots and men would have less time to carve things from wood.

The fur traders show you the goods for which you could trade the furs. You could get iron tools, knives, hatchets, cooking pots, cloth, blankets, glass beads, silver ornaments, guns, and gun powder if you traded furs.

1. How might this hurt your nation if you change your way of hunting?

2. How might this help your nation if you got European goods from the fur traders?

3. Should you trade furs for European goods? Why?

FIGURE 3–3 Students used our original text to discuss Native American perspectives on the fur trade

in the fur trade. We recognized that many Europeans at the time believed Native people were "uncivilized," but we wanted students to think more carefully about this perspective. Ava responded, "I know many people had this view, but what does 'civilized' mean?" Denise explained, "Some may think civilized means one thing while someone else may think civilized means another thing." Ava elaborated, "Native Americans might have thought their lifestyle was very effective for them, why should they change? Are the European goods and way of life more civilized?" Students seemed to think about this idea, but offered no responses.

The group of three Potawatomi students decided they would participate in the fur trade because they could get things they needed from European goods. Although the Ojibwa were concerned about losing their traditional arts through participation in the fur trade, they came up with a plan to keep the basket making tradition alive while still trading pelts and furs. They decided children would learn how to make baskets.

Another undecided group was the Ho-Chunk group of three fourth graders who could not agree on whether the benefits would outweigh the drawbacks if they traded furs for European goods. Judy thought the metal pots would be beneficial while Rameen and Danny were concerned that if they hunt too much, not many animals would be left. They would have little need for metal animal traps, one of the European trade goods. On the other hand, the Menominee decided to participate in the fur trade because they saw the benefits of pots and guns, because guns were easier to use than bows and arrows.

The group of fourth graders then completed research to discover how the Native nation they investigated was involved with and affected by the fur trade. After they read printed resources and took notes, they created charts to summarize in words and drawings at least one benefit to their nation by participation in the fur trade and one harmful effect of the fur trade. Jacob, Patty, and Xee investigated the Menominee and created their chart (see Figure 3–4).

To build on students' ideas from this activity, we created another original text "The Fur Trade," which emphasized Native people's participation in the fur trade. We first read the text aloud to the class, distributed a page of the text to each student to read and illustrate,

HOW THE FUR TRADE HELPED THE NATION	HOW THE FUR TRADE HURT THE NATION
The tribe got different stuff, pots, glass beads, and some blankets.	When the white men came and brought diseases. Many people died.

FIGURE 3–4 Student created chart showing effects of the fur trade on Native people

then read the text again as a class. The text reinforced many of the ideas students developed during their small group discussion, but also included Native people's insistence on quality trade goods and Native women's participation as helpers, guides, interpreters, and wedded partners.[32]

During individual interviews at the close of the unit, the majority of the fourth graders explained what the fur trade was and at least one benefit and drawback of the fur trade for Native people. Students learned European fur traders wanted furs from Native Americans, especially beaver pelts for making beaver hats in demand by wealthy European men. Native Americans obtained such European goods as guns, gun powder, axes, metal pots, knives, cloth, and blankets. Neal summarized what he learned about the fur trade:

> The fur trade was when Europeans came to the Indian tribes and they would trade for guns. A gun would be a couple furs. Then the Indians learned to figure out which ones were good quality and which were poor quality. They only accepted ones that were good quality. When they got that, they could use guns for getting deer instead of bow and arrow. If you shoot a deer with a bow and arrow, it would probably run off. With a gun, if you hit it right where it is supposed to be hit, then it would either fall down immediately or it would just stand there for a couple seconds and then fall down. They traded lead for the guns. Guns, tomahawks, and knives, these didn't come from Indians, they came from Europeans. The Europeans wanted furs, some were really looking for beaver furs. After awhile, they didn't want beaver furs, they wanted silk. So they moved on to somewhere where they had silk.[33]

Students also learned Wisconsin nations benefited from the fur trade. Guns improved men's ability to hunt for food; metal pots made cooking easier for women and reduced the time needed to make their own clay pots and birchbark baskets; and knives allowed women to prepare hides more quickly for clothing. On the other hand, the fur trade harmed Native people because men had to be away from their families to hunt more; the animal population declined because of excessive trapping which affected the food supply; people engaged in traditional crafts such as basketry and pottery less often; there were more conflicts among Europeans and Native nations over the fur trade; and many Native people died from European diseases. Carlos elaborated on the drawbacks and benefits of the fur trade for Native people:

> They would have to go farther and farther away to get the animals they wanted. Sometimes they would fight with the Europeans because they got into disagreements. They would fight with other tribes because they wanted to control the fur trade. The French and Dutch would get into fights over the control of the fur trade, too. The most important thing that affected the Native Americans is that Europeans brought diseases. Most of the Native Americans weren't familiar with the measles, [small]pox and other diseases. Most of the Native Americans died.
>
> They would get guns, just in case they were attacked. They would be able to use their guns. It would be easier to hunt. It would be more effective than a bow and arrow if they ever got in a fight with someone else. The metal pots were easier for the women to cook with, rather than clay pots.[34]

Denise was especially indignant about one harmful effect of the fur trade on Native Americans:

> The Indians would give them [Europeans] so many furs that their food was scarce. They do all this work, they do the fur trade, and all of a sudden, they [Europeans] say, "No, we don't want beaver skin anymore. We like silk caps now." After they hunted all these beavers. The population is almost gone. They say, "No, we don't want them anymore, we want silk hats." Now we can hardly find them anymore and you say, "No, we don't want them anymore."[35]

FOCUS ON YOUR STATE: WHEN NATIVE AMERICANS AND EUROPEANS FIRST MET

Prior to teaching about the initial contact between Native people and Europeans in your own state, you might explore different resources documenting these encounters. Search for different perspectives on the early relationships between these two groups.

• Review authentic resources on Native people in your state (tribal elders, websites, print, and audiovisual materials published or approved by the Native nations) for descriptions of the first contact with Europeans in your state from Native American perspectives. What were the effects of these encounters on Native people? How did Native people benefit from initial contact with Europeans? How were Native people harmed through these encounters? How did Native people treat the first Europeans they met? How did Europeans deal with them?

• Review state historical society resources (guest speakers, children's books, videos, or websites) for European American perspectives on the first contact with Native Americans in your state. Why did the first Europeans enter the area which later became your state? As Europeans pursued their goals, how did they treat Native people? How did Native Americans deal with them? What were the positive and negative outcomes for Europeans as a result of initial contact with Native Americans?

• To bring out diverse perspectives on the initial encounters between Native people and Europeans, you might ask students to read texts, study websites, listen to guest speakers, and view videos of various accounts, summarize the differences with a Venn diagram or chart, or dramatize the diverse perspectives. Encourage your students to question why Native Americans and Europeans viewed the first encounters differently.

INJUSTICES OF TREATIES, RESERVATIONS, AND BOARDING SCHOOLS

Following our study of the fur trade, we introduced students to different perspectives on treaties, treaty rights, reservations, and boarding schools, including the often neglected Native American points of view. The fourth graders also considered cultural and power conflicts between Native people and the U.S. government over land ownership, cultural identity, and Native people's governance. Simulations and readings helped students to understand, empathize with, and become outraged at some of the injustices Native Americans experienced at the hands of the U.S. government.

Standards and Multicultural Themes

The congruence between national, state, and local standards and multicultural themes was especially strong in this part of the curriculum because both emphasized cultural diversity and diverse perspectives. We continued to stress the Culture thematic strand from the national standards, the corresponding Behavioral Sciences: Individuals, Institutions, and Society state and local standards, and the multicultural emphasis on the integration of diverse people's experiences and perspectives in the curriculum.[36] Additionally, we addressed the issue of justice and oppression in the U.S. government's policies and practices in dealing with Native nations, which were part of multicultural education and the national Power, Authority, and Governance thematic strand.[37] The specific state standard included:

• Students will explain the basic purpose of government in American society, recognizing the three levels of government.[38]

We continued to incorporate several school district literacy objectives in our use of readings to introduce students to treaties, treaty rights, reservations, and boarding schools.

Simulations and Readings

Simulations of treaty negotiations and movement to reservations offered students experiences to help them construct an understanding
of some of the complexity and issues surrounding treaties and removal
to reservations. Follow-up class discussions, drawings, journal writing,
and readings were additional strategies to support students' collaborative construction of knowledge of treaties, treaty rights, reservations,
and boarding schools. These strategies are recommended as best teaching practices:

• Form mixed ability groups and have students participate in interactive and cooperative classroom study processes.

• Integrate social studies with other areas of the curriculum.

• Study concepts from different social science disciplines.[39]

Treaties and Treaty Rights

The fourth graders were introduced to differences in Native American and European American cultural values related to land ownership,
which were an important aspect of treaties. Native people maintained
the custom of families having territorial rights to hunt, trap, fish, grow,
and gather food in a specific area.[40] Land was a gift from the Creator
to use respectfully for living. European Americans believed individual
land ownership was highly desirable and a sign of power and wealth.

Students learned that through treaties the Oneida and the
Stockbridge-Munsee band of Mohicans relinquished land in the eastern part of the United States and moved to Wisconsin in the 1820s
while the Menominee, Ho-Chunk, Ojibwa, and Potawatomi ceded
land in Wisconsin. We emphasized the U.S. government's main purpose through treaties was to gain Native people's land for European
American settlement and to allow timber and mining companies to
harvest timber and minerals, such as lead. However, Native people
knew they needed the plant and animal resources from the land to live.

A treaty simulation helped students understand some of the
complexity of the treaty negotiation process between the Menominee,

Ho-Chunk, Ojibwa, and Potawatomi, and the U.S. government. Two-thirds of the class represented the U.S. government, who wanted to purchase the entire state of Wisconsin (represented by the classroom) from the four Native nations. One-third of the class represented the four Native nations who were unwilling to sell the entire state (or classroom), but would allow the U.S. government to use certain areas. The students portraying the Wisconsin Native nations sat at one table in the front of the classroom while those representing the U.S. government sat at a table in the back. They had to discuss and decide on offers and counteroffers by consensus. However, only their interpreters and negotiators made offers to and responded to offers from the other group.

To begin the simulation, representatives from both groups met in the center of the classroom. The U.S. government negotiator and interpreter first asked the Native nations for all the land (the classroom) in exchange for six desks. After consulting with the remaining Native people, the Native American negotiator and interpreter refused this offer and counteroffered with giving half the land in exchange for silk cloth, four guns, 20 pounds of lead, three axes, and four governmental officials to work for Native people. The government negotiator and interpreter took this offer to their group, then presented a different offer. Native nations could keep the closet, the desks, and the government would provide two government members to work for Native people. The Native American negotiator and interpreter astutely questioned, "What do the desks do?" After the government interpreter and negotiator explained, "They help your children learn," the Native American response was, "We have to think about it." At this point, we ended the simulation due to time constraints, but the follow-up discussion illustrated students' understanding of the difficulty of treaty negotiations. They knew the process of reaching a consensus with other members of their group was time consuming and talking through interpreters could lead to misunderstandings between the two groups. Many understood Wisconsin Native people were at a disadvantage because treaty negotiations were conducted through interpreters and final treaties were written in English, which Native Americans could not read. Maria, a member of the Native nations during the simulation, summarized what she gained from the experience in her journal:

> It was very hard to think of things so they [U.S. government] could agree with us because the U.S. government wanted all the land when we had the land first, we shoud just give them a quarter of the room if they had all the land and we get 5 or 6 desks that wouldn't be fair because they would probably give us worthless stuff like broken guns, teared silk cloth, and just 15 lbs. of lead than 20 lbs. of lead. If I were a real Native American then I would be really mad at the U.S. government for wanting all the land when we got it first.

Through reading and dramatizing summaries of treaties negotiated between the Menominee, Ho-Chunk, and the U.S. government described at the beginning of the chapter, we hoped students would learn how Native people were often lied to, coerced into signing treaties, paid little for the land, and forced off their land even when they did not understand the final treaty. We divided students into three groups. Each group read a published summary of the treaty negotiations and final treaty for either the Menominee or Ho-Chunk,[41] decided how they would dramatize the main events in the negotiations and final treaty, then presented their dramatization to the class.

Students learned that the Wisconsin tribes wanted to keep their land for living and hunting or were willing to share their land with the government. They understood some of the challenges of treaty negotiations, including that Native people and the U.S. government had different desires for the land, they spoke different languages, and they couldn't agree on terms. Students cited issues of injustice related to treaties as the government tricked or lied to Native people, the Native Americans could not read the treaties and did not know what they said, tribal representatives were forced to sign the treaties, Native people were compelled to move from land they had lived on all their lives, the government claimed ownership of most of the land originally belonging to the Native Americans, and Native people were forced to move to small reservations. By examining maps of where Native nations lived in Wisconsin at different times, students recognized Native people lived all over the state in the early 1800s, but now lived on significantly smaller reservations. Judy's journal indicated her understanding:

I learned that treaty means agreement. I learned that if you were a Native American or part of one of the Wisconsin tribes it would have been verey hard to live through what happend because who wants thier land that they live on took away? I know I wouldn't. For the u.s. government it was grate because they were getting land to live on.

Treaty rights have been a controversial issue within Wisconsin, with violent protests over a decade ago when Ojibwa bands exercised treaty rights to fish. By reading and discussing Ojibwa treaty rights,[42] students understood these included the right to hunt, fish, and gather plants for their food, clothing, and medicine and why they were so important for Ojibwa people's survival. Most students recognized the Ojibwa people needed treaty rights in order to have enough food to live.

During individual interviews at the end of the unit, most students understood what treaties were, who negotiated them, and the U.S. government's intention to obtain land through treaties. They also explained why treaties were unfair for Native people. Charlotte elaborated on the meaning of treaties:

> They [treaties] were an agreement over the land the Indians had. The Indians had to go to the capital of the United States, Washington, DC to see the President about the treaties. Most Indians didn't know what they really said. Then they [governmental officials] would come to take over the land and the Indians would be like, "What are you doing?" because they really didn't know what the treaties said. The Indians got mad after they saw what was happening. They thought the treaties said something different than what they said. The government wanted land from the Indians. The Indians said, "Well, if you have this land, then we need to get something back for this." They negotiated between the two. They had translators that had to go back and forth to each other. The Indians would say, "What would you give us for this land?" Then they would have to decide. It would just go back and forth until they reached an agreement they liked.[43]

Treaty rights were clarified by many students, including Rameen. "I learned that Ojibwa had a treaty right that they could hunt, fish, and gather, even if they sold their land. If they couldn't hunt, fish, or gather, then they would die because they wouldn't have any food to keep them alive."[44]

Reservations

A simulation of the Menominee, Ho-Chunk, Ojibwa, and Potawatomi removal to reservations in Wisconsin (the Ho-Chunk never had reservation lands in Wisconsin, but have several communities) was very powerful in helping students think about justice issues related to reservations and whose interests the U.S. government represented when they forced Native people in our state to move to reservations. While the students were at lunch, we moved their desks to a limited space in the classroom and marked the boundary with masking tape, which represented a reservation's borders. When the fourth graders entered the classroom, we explained they had to sit in their desks on the reservation and could not leave the reservation to use any other resources in the classroom, representing the state of Wisconsin.

To our delight, Susan asked, "What about treaty rights?" After encouraging Susan to elaborate on her idea, she added, "If you were Ojibwa, you would have treaty rights and could use the land." Thelma questioned, "Was it only the Ojibwa?" Then Ava asked, "What did they [Ojibwa] have the right to do?" Carlos responded, "Even though they sold the land, they could still hunt, fish, and gather," and Patty added, "They could still get things they needed to survive from the land they sold." We clarified that those students representing the Ojibwa could get resources from the rest of the classroom during this activity, but the other nations did not have treaty rights. When Patty commented, "You could ask them to get you something," we explained, "The Ojibwa got treaty rights for their own survival. They weren't supposed to sell them to other people."

In order to help students develop a greater understanding of reservations, we asked students to read and discuss an original summary we created of what reservations were like for Native people. A copy of this can be seen in Figure 3–5. In addition, we read aloud descriptions of reservation life for the Ojibwa and Menominee.[45]

WHAT WERE RESERVATIONS LIKE FOR NATIVE PEOPLE?

By the late 1800s, almost every Native nation in the United States had been assigned to a reservation. Reservations are areas of land set aside by the government for use by Native people. Native Americans did not want to live on reservations. They preferred living their traditional lifestyle. After many Native nations lost their homelands through treaties, they agreed to live on reservations.

The U.S. government agreed not to remove Native people from these reservations. However, the U.S. government created reservations so they could control Native people's lives and prevent them from practicing many of their traditions. The government also wanted to isolate Native people from European American people. Native Americans could no longer decide where and how they should live.

Reservations were controlled by Indian agents. These people made many decisions about the Native people's lives who lived on reservations. Native people were told how to dress, what religion to practice, what kind of farming to do, and where their children should attend school. The U.S. government often sent food and clothing to reservations which were of poor quality. There was not always enough food and clothing for everyone.

For many years, this was a bad time for Native people. They became dependent on the government for providing what they needed to live. Many Native people could no longer get the food, clothing, and housing they needed through traditional ways. Native Americans lost part of their culture and pride in being Native American.

The Menominee, Ojibway, Potawatomi, Stockbridge-Munsee, and Oneida have reservations in Wisconsin today. The Ho-Chunk have communities in Wisconsin, but no reservation.

FIGURE 3–5 Original summary of reservation life for the simulation

Finally, as a class we reviewed what was learned about reservations from the simulation. Students recorded in their journals their ideas about how Native Americans might have felt about being removed to and living on reservations The students used words and drawings to illustrate what reservations were like for Native people for a class collage, as shown in Figure 3–6. Hua recorded her feelings about the simulation in her journal:

> I feel sad during the simulation because we were all crowed [crowded] in a land that was small. I think Native Americans felt mad because Europeans were taking over their land and they had to live on reser-

FIGURE 3–6 Collage students created illustrating characteristics of Native people's reservations

vations. The reservations had bad farming land and the government picked what they had to wear their clothes, farm what land, eat what, and practice what religion.

Xee's journal also reflected the understanding that reservations were restrictive for Native people, especially if they did not have treaty rights:

> I felt afule [awful] because we are scruched up like one tribe. It is bad because we can't go anywhere because we are on the reservation, so we can't get to the bathroom on time. Only the Ojibway can get out of the reservation because they had a treaty right so they can go out of the reservation. I think they felt mad because they wanted to live in there own livestyle and pratice their tarditions and other stuff. And they want to wear their own clothes and do what they wanted to do. They want to live in their own homes, like wigams and long house.

The simulation helped students learn about some of the difficulties the Native nations experienced in surviving on reservations, including the reservation's smaller area than their traditional lands, their limitations on growing and hunting food on the reduced land area, the poor quality of the land, the forced change to European American food, housing, and clothing, and restrictions on practicing their religion. During interviews at the close of the unit, students elaborated on their understanding of reservations and the injustices Native people experienced on reservations.

> The Ojibwa had treaty rights so they could hunt, gather, and fish on their land. Other tribes were forced to sign treaties, so they had to move to reservations. The U.S. government would send them little bits of food like pork. They usually didn't eat pork, so they didn't know what to do with it. They felt bad because they had to give up their land and move to reservations and different states they didn't know. I don't think it was fair at all because when they moved to reservations they couldn't practice their own religion. They had to stop making most of their traditional crafts. They didn't get that much food. The Native American people were told how to dress, what religion to practice, what kind of farming to do, and where they should attend school.[46]

Boarding Schools

Reading aloud the picture books *Cheyenne Again* and *The Ledgerbook of Thomas Blue Eagle*[47] introduced students to Native American children's boarding school experiences. Both texts portray a young Cheyenne or Lakota boy's attendance at a boarding school far away from his family. Although we could not find trade books depicting Wisconsin Native American children's boarding school experiences, the descriptions in *Cheyenne Again* and *The Ledgerbook of Thomas Blue Eagle* appeared very similar. We considered *The Ledgerbook of Thomas Blue Eagle* an authentic portrayal because the authors consulted with a Lakota historian and educator in preparing the book. The power of each boy's story embellished with excellent illustrations seemed to move the students to empathize with the main characters and develop an understanding of the injustices Native children experienced at boarding schools.

The texts helped students learn that most Native children did not want to attend boarding schools, their parents did not want them to attend, or their parents had conflicting views on their children's attendance at boarding schools. Our students were indignant that Native children were encouraged to give up their culture and adopt European American culture at boarding schools. They were forced to wear school uniforms rather than their traditional clothing. Their hair was cut in conflict with the cultural tradition to cut their hair only at the deaths of family members. Native children were forced to speak only English and forbidden to speak their first language. They studied Christianity and were not allowed to practice their own religion. Native students learned European American versions of history rather than Native American historical stories. School officials gave Native children new names and did not address them by the name the students earned in their family or nation.

In interviews at the close of the unit, most students learned that boarding schools took Native American students from their families and the children were forced to give up some of their culture while attending the schools. Patty provided a very detailed explanation of the intentions and practices of boarding schools:

The Native Americans that lived in the North went to the West boarding schools. The Native Americans from the West went to the East boarding schools because the Europeans wanted them to be as far away from home so they wouldn't run away. They also wanted them to go to boarding schools because they wanted them to learn the American ways. They wanted them to forget their own ways. One of their traditions was if someone dies, you have to cut your hair. But when they went there [boarding school], they thought people had died in their family because they got their hair cut. But really, that was just what the Europeans wanted them to do. They have to learn English. They have to speak English. They usually went to boarding schools in their best dressed clothes, but when they got there, they had to wear European clothes. They had to dress in cloth instead of deerskin.[48]

FOCUS ON YOUR STATE: TREATIES, RESERVATIONS, AND BOARDING SCHOOLS

In preparation for developing your own teaching strategies addressing specific treaties, treaty rights, reservations, and boarding schools in your state, contact your state's Native nations and historical societies for resources to help your students investigate:

• What happened during treaty negotiations between Native nations in your state and the U.S. government? What did Native people relinquish and acquire as a result of these treaties? How fair were these treaties? Which Native nations in your state have treaty rights? What are these rights?

• Where are Native American reservations located in your state (for a map of reservations in the U.S., see the website *www.nativeamericanonline.com*)? Why might they be located there? How do Native people feel about their reservations? What are the benefits and drawbacks of living on a reservation for Native Americans? How did the U.S. government and European American immigrants benefit from reservations?

For general resources dealing with treaties, reservations, and boarding schools across different states, you might use:

• The children's picture book, *The People Shall Continue*,[49] is an excellent overview of the traditional lives of all Native American nations, the struggle over land between Native people and Europeans, the treaties which resulted in Native nations' movement to reservations, and Native children's separation from their families by attending boarding schools.

• The texts *Native American FAQs Handbook* and *Indian Treaties*[50] offer additional background information on the unfairness of treaties and treaty negotiations for Native people.

• The children's picture books *Cheyenne Again*, *The Ledgerbook of Thomas Blue Eagle*, and *Jim Thorpe Young Athlete*[51] provide portrayals of many different Native children's boarding school experiences. The last text describes a Sac and Fox boy's boarding school experiences in Oklahoma, Kansas, and Pennsylvania.

CURRENT TRENDS TOWARD SELF-DETERMINATION AND FIGHTING RACISM

Our final focus for the unit was providing opportunities for the fourth graders to understand the concept of Native American self-determination, a current movement for Native nations gaining sovereignty, self-government, and control over their own lives rather than depending on the U.S. government. Although self-determination is a very challenging concept to teach fourth graders, we provided opportunities for students to collaborate in constructing an understanding. We also wanted students to become more aware of racist oppression Native people experience today and ways the students themselves might fight against racism.

Addressing Standards and Multicultural Themes

We continued to address the national *Culture; Time, Continuity, and Change; and Power, Authority and Governance* thematic strands and the corresponding state and local standards. Also integrated within the curriculum were the multicultural themes of including different cultural group's experiences and perspectives and addressing social issues such as racism.[52] Literacy was integrated with social studies, a best teaching practice,[53] and class discussions were used to provide opportunities for students to construct knowledge together.[54]

Self-Determination and the Milwaukee Indian Community School

The concept of self-determination was explored primarily through the well-illustrated trade book *One Nation, Many Tribes: How Kids Live in Milwaukee's Indian Community.*[55] The text introduced our students to the Milwaukee Indian Community School, which admitted only Native American students. The school affirmed cultural diversity and countered racism directed against Native people by teaching the cultures and histories of Wisconsin Native Americans and fostering a sense of pride in being Native American. The text focused on two contemporary Ojibwa youth who attended the school, learned about the culture and history of the Wisconsin nations, and participated in the school's cultural activities. The characters described the value of learning about their own culture and history at the school and their reactions to prejudicial comments from non-Native people when they danced at powwows. Through the characters, we were briefly introduced to current issues among Native people, the use of Native American names for sports teams or commercial products and poverty on reservations.

The fourth graders chose how they wanted to read the text, either alone, with a partner, with an audiotaped version, or with one of us. After they read the text, they recorded their responses to questions about the reading in their journals, and we discussed as a class what they learned from their reading. During one of our class discussions, students spontaneously began comparing differences between the Milwaukee Indian Community School and earlier boarding schools Native children were forced to attend. The fourth graders distinguished the disparity between boarding schools' intention to assimilate Native children into European American culture and the Milwaukee Indian Community School's goal to strengthen Native American cultural identity and pride.

Denise said, "They really wanted them to learn about their ancestors, that's really different from boarding schools. In boarding schools they never learn that way. Now they're saying, 'we want you to learn as much as you can.'" Danny added, "They got to see their parents more at the community school than they did at the boarding school"; and Rameen offered, "Mom and Dad in the other story said they didn't want them to go [to boarding school]; in this story they did want them to go." Jacob continued, "They didn't have to sleep at this school." Carlos suggested, "If they ran away from school or did something wrong, they wouldn't have to get a chain wrapped around their leg." Rameen said, "The teachers there were nice. They have Indian teachers." Danny continued, "Teachers at this school wanted them to keep their traditions" and Carlos added, "The teachers wouldn't call them dumb or anything."

Racism and Fourth Graders

During another class discussion, we raised the issue of prejudice and discrimination toward Native Americans, particularly the main characters portrayed in *One Nation, Many Tribes: How Kids Live in Milwaukee's Indian Community*. We wanted our students to consider ways they could take action against unfair treatment or oppression directed at Native people. Ava read the passage in the text in which one main character, Thirza, complained that non-Native kids made war whoops when she did hoop dancing. She asked the fourth graders to consider what they could do if Thirza and Shawnee came to our school and danced and others ridiculed them. Charlotte suggested, "We could give them some positive compliments on their dancing." Carlos added, "If someone were teasing them, we could tell them to stop;"

and Judy suggested, "You could ask them to realize they're people too and think of how you would feel in this situation." Denise offered, "Ask a couple of people if they would go up to them and give them compliments so people teasing them would see, 'I guess they're not so bad'" and "If someone were making fun, I would say, 'I would like it very much if you would apologize.'" Following this discussion, we asked students to create a class book portraying how we could become friends with someone from a different culture, such as Shawnee and Thirza, and counter any discrimination they might endure at our school. Each fourth grader created a page for a class book, shown in Figure 3–7, illustrating how they would extend friendship if Shawnee and Thirza came to our school and stand up to any racism they experienced.

During individual interviews at the close of the unit, most students understood how the Milwaukee Indian Community School helped Wisconsin Native people move toward self-determination by teaching tribal histories, cultures, and traditions at the school. They learned how the school taught powwow dances, Native American history, languages, and religions to Native children and provided

If Thirza and Shawnee came to this school I would be a friend to them like any other human being.

FIGURE 3–7 One of the pages students created for the *Welcome Thirza and Shawnee* class book

opportunities for Native children to engage in cultural traditions, such as the sweat lodge and pipe ceremony. A majority of the fourth graders also became more aware of current issues for Native people today, such as the use of Indian names for sports teams or products, the ridicule directed at Native Americans while they dance at pow-wows, and poverty on reservations. Charlotte elaborated:

> Shawnee and Thirza were mad because we would make fun of them, call them names, make jokes, and they don't like that. They also don't like that we put the Indians on reservations and left them with nothing there. We just gave them a little house and some land. They wished they had grocery stores and banks. They didn't like at the dances, when they were dancing, that we would come around and make Indian noises like you hear on tv. They know a lot of that stuff isn't true. They just make that up on tv. Most people like us believe that is the way Indians are. But they know the truth. That really isn't the real thing. They are trying to raise money to make a good life for themselves, even though they have to live on reservations.[56]

FOCUS ON YOUR STATE: CURRENT ISSUES AMONG NATIVE AMERICANS

In order to introduce your students to the most authentic resources on Native American contemporary concerns, such as political sovereignty, cultural preservation, and economic improvements, you might:

• Invite Native American guest speakers from your state. The guest speakers could explain what the present issues are for Native people and why they are so important.

• If guest speakers are not available, contact Native American people or organizations in your state for suggestions of websites, videos, and print materials such as children's books which elaborate on current concerns of Native people in your state.

For general resources dealing with current issues for Native people, see *Native American FAQs Handbook*, *Native Americans Today: Resources and Activities for Educators Grades 4–8*, and *Teaching About Native Americans*.[57] These texts provide background information, lesson plans, and instructional resources for teaching about contemporary concerns among Native Americans from many different nations.

REFLECTIONS AND RECOMMENDATIONS

We were very satisfied with the fourth graders' openness to learning about, respecting, and appreciating the traditional lifestyles and changes Wisconsin Native nations experienced as a result of the fur trade and the hardships resulting from treaties, removal to reservations, and forced attendance at boarding schools. Students developed an understanding of some of the cultural values which are the basis for the traditional lifestyles of the Menominee, Ho-Chunk, Ojibwa, Potawatomi, Oncida, and the Stockbridge-Munsee band of Mohicans and their current efforts to continue traditions and reclaim sovereignty. We encourage you to not only introduce your students to Native nations who lived in your state at any time, but go beyond a superficial focus on lifestyles to the cultural values which influenced lifestyles. It is also important to address the more challenging aspects of Native American history in your state, including the relationships with the U.S. government and European immigrants. By addressing the topics of treaties, reservations, and boarding schools, your students will have opportunities to examine conflicts among groups, how these conflicts were resolved in the past, and how they could be more fairly resolved in the future.

Even though we were pleased with the credibility of the print resources we used, we continue to search for additional guest speakers, especially elders from several Native nations to teach each nation's history, culture, and cultural values. We have been fortunate to have a Menominee woman who provides valuable insights on some of the cultural beliefs and traditions associated with powwows. By inviting elders from several Native nations to help teach the unit, you are using Native American oral traditions for teaching each nation's history and culture. We encourage you to draw on elders' knowledge of important cultural traditions and values, Native people's perspectives on the fur trade, conflicts over land, treaties, treaty rights, reservations, boarding schools, and the significance of self-determination for Native people today.

ENDNOTES

1. Jane A. Hieb, *Visions and Voices: Winnebago Elders Speak to the Children* (Independence, WI: Western Dairyland Economic Opportunity Council, 1994) 38–46.
2. Howard W. Kanetzke, "Oshkosh and Menominee Lands," *Badger History* 29 No. 4 (March 1976): 56–60. Although no longer in print, *Badger History* was a publication designed for fourth graders to use in learning Wisconsin history and published by the State Historical Society of Wisconsin.
3. National Council for the Social Studies, *Expectations of Excellence: Curriculum Standards for Social Studies* (Washington, DC: National Council for the Social Studies, 1994), 49.
4. Hal Balsiger, Paula DeHart, Margaret A. Laughlin, Stephen A. Rose, and Michael Yell, *Planning Curriculum in Social Studies* (Madison, WI: Wisconsin Department of Public Instruction, 2001), 117.
5. National Council for the Social Studies, 54.
6. Balsiger et al., 40.
7. Christine A. Sleeter and Carl A. Grant, *Making Choices for Multicultural Education: Five Approaches to Race, Class, and Gender,* 3rd ed. (Upper Saddle River, NJ: Merrill, 1999), 188–216.
8. Each group contained girls and boys, varied achievement levels, and, when possible, different cultural backgrounds. We placed two Hmong students with limited English skills in groups with another Hmong student proficient in both English and Hmong who could discuss ideas in Hmong.
9. Steven Zemelman, Harvey Daniels, and Arthur Hyde, *Best Practice: New Standards for Teaching and Learning in America's Schools* (Portsmouth, NH: Heinemann, 1998), 132–155.
10. Gloria Ladson-Billings, "But That's Just Good Teaching! The Case for Culturally Relevant Pedagogy," *Theory Into Practice* 34 (1995), 159–165; Valerie O. Pang and Robertta H. Barba, "The Power of Culture: Building Culturally Affirming Instruction," in Carl A. Grant, ed., *Educating*

for Diversity: An Anthology of Multicultural Voices (Boston: Allyn and Bacon, 1995), 341–358.

11. Carrie Rothstein-Fisch, Patricia M. Greenfield, and Elise Trumball, "Bridging Cultures with Classroom Strategies," *Educational Leadership* 56 (1999), 64–67.

12. Bonnie Shemie, *Houses of Bark: Tipi, Wigwam, and Longhouse* (Montreal: Tundra Books, 1990); Jill Duvall, *The Oneida* (Chicago: Childrens Press, 1991); Joan Kalbacken, *The Menominee* (Chicago: Childrens Press, 1994); Eileen Lucas, *The Ojibwas: People of the Northern Forests* (Brookfield, CT: Millbrook, 1994); Alice Osinski, *The Chippewa* (Chicago: Childrens Press, 1987); Jane A. Hieb, *Visions and Voices: Winnebago Elders Speak to the Children* (Independence, WI: Western Dairyland Economic Opportunity Council, 1994); Chet Kozlak, *Ojibway Indians Coloring Book* (St. Paul, MN: Minnesota Historical Society, 1979); American Indian Language and Culture Education Board, *The History of the Hochungra People: Winnebago Tribe of Wisconsin* (Madison, WI: Author, n.d.); Shelley Oxley, *The Anishinabe: An Overview Unit of the History and Background of the Wisconsin Ojibway Indian Tribe* (Madison, WI: American Indian Language and Culture Education Board, 1981); Stockbridge-Munsee Historical Committee, *The History of the Stockbridge-Munsee Band of Mohican Indians*, 2nd ed. (Bowler, WI: Muh-He-Con-Neew Press, 1993); Shelley Oxley, *The History of the Menominee Indians* (Madison, WI: American Indian Language and Culture Education Board, 1981); Shelley Oxley, *The History of the Oneida Indians* (Madison, WI: American Indian Language and Culture Education Board, 1981); Shelley Oxley, *Keepers of the Fire: The History of the Potawatomi Indians of Wisconsin* (Madison, WI: American Indian Language and Culture Education Board, 1981).

13. Interview with Mandy, 11/18/97.

14. Interview with Charlotte, 11/4/97.

15. Interview with Denise, 11/6/97.

16. Gordon Regguinti, *The Sacred Harvest: Ojibway Wild Rice Gathering* (Minneapolis, MN: Lerner, 1992).

17. Laura Waterman Wittstock, *Ininatig's Gift of Sugar: Traditional Native Sugarmaking* (Minneapolis, MN: Lerner, 1993).

18. Sally M. Hunter, *Four Seasons of Corn: A Winnebago Tradition* (Minneapolis, MN: Lerner, 1997).

19. Interview with Denise, 11/6/97.

20. Marcie R. Rendon, *Powwow Summer: A Family Celebrates the Circle of Life* (Minneapolis, MN: Carolrhoda Books, 1996).

113

21. Sandra King, *Shannon: An Ojibway Dancer* (Minneapolis, MN: Lerner, 1993).
22. Joe McLellan, *Nanabosho Dances* (Winnipeg, Canada: Pemmican Publications, 1991).
23. Interview with Denise, 11/6/97.
24. Beverly Slapin and Doris Seale, eds., *Through Indian Eyes: The Native Experience in Books for Children* (Berkeley, CA: Oyate, 1998).
25. Arlene Hirschfelder and Yvonne Beamer, *Native Americans Today: Resources and Activities for Educators Grades 4–8* (Englewood, CO: Teacher Ideas Press, 2000); Karen D. Harvey, Lisa D. Harjo, and Jane K. Jackson, *Teaching About Native Americans*, 2nd ed. (Washington DC: National Council for the Social Studies, 1997); Karen D. Harvey, Lisa D. Harjo, and Lynda Welborn, *How to Teach About American Indians: A Guide for the School Library Media Specialist* (Westport, CT: Greenwood Press, 1995).
26. Sleeter and Grant, 189.
27. Balsiger et al., 117.
28. National Council for the Social Studies, 51.
29. Balsiger et al., 61–62.
30. This narrative was based largely on articles in the June, 1982, issue of *Cobblestone* which focused on the theme "The North American Beaver Trade."
31. Russell W. Fridley and Jean A. Brookins, J. A., *Where the Two Worlds Meet: The Great Lakes Fur Trade* (St. Paul, MN: Minnesota Historical Society, 1982), 57; Chet Kozlak, *A Great Lakes Fur Trade Coloring Book* (St. Paul, MN: Minnesota Historical Society, 1981), 5, 9–10.
32. John Demos, *The Tried and the True: Native American Women Confronting Colonization* (New York: Oxford University Press, 1995), 59–73; Jack Rudolph, "The Beaver Trade," *Cobblestone* 3 (June 1982): 9–13.
33. Interview with Neal, 11/12/97.
34. Interview with Carlos, 11/4/97.
35. Interview with Denise, 11/6/97.
36. Sleeter and Grant, 189.
37. National Council for the Social Studies, 63.
38. Balsiger et al., 78.
39. Zemelman et al., 132–155.
40. Alec Paul, "Our Stock of Food and Clothes," in Peter Nabokov, ed., *Native American Testimony: A Chronicle of Indian-White Relations from*

Prophecy to the Present, 1492–2000, rev. ed. (New York: Penguin, 1999) 85–87.

41. Kanetzke, "Oshkosh and Menominee Lands;" Howard W. Kanetzke, "Wa Kun Cha Koo Kah, Yellow Thunder," *Badger History* 29 No. 4 (March 1976): 61–64; Hieb, 38–46.

42. Sue Erickson, *Chippewa Treaties: Understanding and Impact*, 2nd ed. (Odanah, WI: Great Lakes Indian Fish and Wildlife Commission, 1994), 8–9.

43. Interview with Charlotte, 12/16/97.

44. Interview with Rameen, 12/3/97.

45. Helen Hornbeck Tanner, *The Ojibwa* (New York: Chelsea House, 1992), 83–84; Patricia K. Ourada, *The Menominee* (New York: Chelsea House, 1990), 59.

46. Interview with Carlos, 12/4/97.

47. Eve Bunting, *Cheyenne Again* (New York: Clarion, 1995); Gay Matthaei and Jewel H. Grutman, *The Ledgerbook of Thomas Blue Eagle* (New York: Lickle, 1994).

48. Interview with Patty, 12/3/97.

49. Simon Ortiz, *The People Shall Continue* (San Francisco, CA: Children's Book Press, 1988).

50. George Russell, *Native American FAQs Handbook* (Phoenix, AZ: Russell Publications, 2000), 35–37; Susan Dudley Gold, *Indian Treaties* (New York: Twenty-First Century Books, 1997).

51. Bunting; Matthai and Grutman; Laurence Santrey, *Jim Thorpe Young Athlete* (Mahwah, NJ: Troll Associates, 1983).

52. Sleeter and Grant, 189.

53. Zemelman et al., 132–155.

54. Jere Brophy and Janet Alleman, *Powerful Social Studies for Elementary Students* (New York: Harcourt Brace, 1996), 63–77; Geoffrey Scheurman, "From Behaviorist to Constructivist Teaching," *Social Education* 62 (1998), 6–9.

55. Kathleen Krull, *One Nation, Many Tribes: How Kids Live in Milwaukee's Indian Community* (New York: Lodestar Books, 1995).

56. Interview with Charlotte, 12/26/97.

57. Russell, 83–114; Hirschfelder and Beamer, 191–207; Harvey, Harjo, and Jackson, 55–63.

CHAPTER 4

EXPLORING DIVERSE PERSPECTIVES
ON BECOMING A STATE AND ON
VOTING RIGHTS

In the front of the classroom, two members of the Menominee family, Xee and Susan, played the role of the U.S. government, while the remaining two, Judy and John, dramatized the Menominee. The students make up one of the family groups who assumed a specific identity with different perspectives on Wisconsin becoming a state. The families included two of the indigenous nations, the Ho-Chunk and Menominee, and different immigrant groups: poor English miners, wealthy German Americans, land-owning "Yankees,"[1] and struggling German immigrants. The families read about and summarized what their lives were like when Wisconsin was part of the Northwest Territory and later became a separate territory. With guidance from us, each family chose how to share summaries with the class. Both the Menominee and wealthy German American families decided to dramatize their lifestyle.

Xee and Susan carried suitcases and asked Judy and John, "Can we have your land?" However, Judy and John refused and explained, "Because it's our land." The government leaders promised, "We'll give you that much area over there" and pointed to a small portion of the classroom by the windows. Then one government official said to another, "We should send them to Minnesota and see if they like it. I'll go write a treaty." However, the Menominee family members were not happy with the land in Minnesota and explained, "It was too small." When Xee and Susan presented the paper (treaty) for Judy and John to sign, the Menominee asked, "What's it for?" and then signed it without hearing an explanation. The government officials jumped up and down and exclaimed, "Yes, we got their land!" They said to the Menominee, "You signed a treaty, get out, we said you have to stay in this area" (again pointing to a small portion of the classroom). As they moved to the "reservation" area of the classroom, the Menominee family members consoled themselves with, "At least we have some land rather than none."

A very different dramatization was presented by the wealthy German American family, as shown in Figure 4–1. The first scene showed the family at home. Danny questioned his father, "Dad, are you going to vote today?" Hua, who played the role of the father, replied, "Yes, I am, because it's very important to vote." Danny then asked, "Why won't they let Mom vote?" Patty, playing the role of the mother, immediately lamented, "I wish I could vote, but they won't let me. I don't know why. I don't think it's fair that the father can vote but I can't. But, anyway, I have to keep an eye on the 'hands' and the girls (hired workers)." In the next scene, Danny played the role of an election official who questioned Hua, as the German American father arrived at the polls to vote. "Are you here to vote?" asked Danny. Hua replied, "Yes, I am." After Hua marked her ballot and

FIGURE 4–1 The wealthy German American family dramatize their lifestyle prior to statehood

handed it to the poll official, she observed, "Why aren't there many people here to vote today?" Danny responded, "Because not many people own much land." Apparently satisfied with the explanation, the wealthy German American farmer replied, "I'm going home to look over my five hundred acres of land."

This scene from our state government unit illustrated our focus on encouraging the fourth graders to understand that there were many different perspectives regarding Wisconsin becoming a separate territory and eventually a state. We were especially concerned that the students learn the process of becoming a state was not an inevitable sequence of events, but rather resulted from efforts of the U.S. government and wealthy male land owners to increase their power in a sparsely settled part of the continent. By assuming the identity of family members from different cultural and socioeconomic backgrounds, the fourth graders for a short time walked in the shoes of the state's indigenous people as well as recent and established immigrants as they learned about becoming a state and the voting rights of diverse groups.

DIFFERENT PERSPECTIVES ON LIFE BEFORE STATEHOOD

Standards and Multicultural Ideas

When we introduced students to life in the region during 1787–1848, when the state was still part of the Northwest Territory and then a separate territory, we integrated national, state, and local social studies standards with multicultural themes. We focused on the national social studies thematic strand of Power, Authority, and Governance.[2] Our goal was for students to learn about the evolution of government as Wisconsin moved from being part of the Northwest Territory to a separate territory, how government met the needs of different groups of people, and ways government promoted the power of some groups while diminishing the power of others. We encouraged students to analyze when the government treated people fairly and when it was unjust. The national thematic strand corresponded to the state and local Political Science and Citizenship standard:

• Students will explain the basic purpose of government in American society, recognizing the three levels of government.[3]

For the Civic Ideals and Practices[4] national thematic strand, we provided opportunities for students to learn about the rights and responsibilities different groups had in the state, especially voting, and actions people can take to influence governmental decisions, such as voting. Our attention to the national standard also allowed us to address the local and state Political Science and Citizenship standard:

• Students will explain how various forms of civic action such as running for political office, voting, signing an initiative, and speaking at hearings can contribute to the well-being of the community.[5]

These standards were very congruent with the multicultural education emphasis on introducing different cultural group's experiences and perspectives and organizing content around such social issues as racism, classism, and sexism.[6] By asking students to assume a family's specific cultural and socioeconomic identity as the lens through which they examined life in the Northwest Territory and the Wisconsin Territory, we hoped the fourth graders would bring out the very diverse perspectives indigenous people and European immigrants might have held. We also asked students to examine the sexism, racism, and classism implied by questioning who benefited and who did not among women, men, Native people, European Americans, wealthy land owners, and poor immigrants living in the area when Wisconsin became a part of the Northwest Territory, a separate territory, and eventually a state.

Small Group Discussions: Best Teaching Practices and Culturally Relevant, Social Constructivist Methods

In order to build on the cultural value of cooperation,[7] promote the engagement and success of the English language learners, and encourage students to collaboratively construct knowledge[8] about life in Wisconsin before it became a state, we divided the fourth graders into heterogeneous small groups or families. Each group had a distinct family identity based on our research of different groups who lived in the region before statehood.[9] Because we could find no appropriate text for students, we created original, brief descriptions of life in the Northwest Territory and the Wisconsin Territory, a copy of which can be seen in Figure 4–2. Next, from the perspective of their own family identity, each small group read, discussed the summaries, and

WHAT WAS IT LIKE TO LIVE IN THE WISCONSIN TERRITORY FROM 1836 UNTIL 1848?

The first step for Wisconsin to become a separate territory was when the President and Congress appointed a governor, secretary, and three judges. However, the only people who could become these leaders were men who owned at least five hundred acres of land. The governor and judges made all the laws.

The second step for Wisconsin to become a separate territory was when there were five thousand voters living in the area. A voter was a free man who was at least twenty-one years old. He must own fifty acres of land and have lived in the area for at least two years. Women, people who could not afford to own land, people who worked for someone else, escaped slaves, free African Americans, and Native Americans were not voters. Voters could elect the legislature or the people who made laws for the territory. The legislature was made up of the Upper House or Senate and Lower House or Assembly. Voters also elected a delegate to Congress in Washington, DC, but he could not vote with other members of Congress.

Some European Americans and European immigrants did not want Wisconsin to become a territory. This would mean Wisconsin would be separate from the Northwest Territory and have its own government. They did not want the government telling them what to do. They also did not want to pay taxes to support the government.

Native Americans had nothing to gain from Wisconsin becoming a territory and much to lose. As more and more European Americans moved into the area, it was more difficult for them to hold onto their lands. Native people could not vote, saw no need for the territorial government, and did not want to pay taxes to support this government.

(continues)

Some European Americans wanted Wisconsin to become a territory because they wanted their own governor and wanted Wisconsin to become a state.

Wisconsin became a territory in 1836 and President Andrew Jackson appointed Henry Dodge as the territorial governor. The Wisconsin territory government became busy organizing county and city governments and deciding on taxes. The government also tried to make it easier for European Americans and European immigrants to live in Wisconsin by building roads, harbors, and dams. The government began organizing free public schools and hired teachers for schools. However, roads during this time were poor. People developed stagecoach routes and built simple inns along the routes. The government also tried to improve mail service for people by developing weekly mail routes and setting up post offices.

Many European Americans, or Yankee immigrants from eastern states such as New York or New England states, and new immigrants from Europe moved into the Wisconsin territory. The Germans were the largest group of immigrants. The English, Scots, Welsh, and Irish formed another large group. After they moved into the Wisconsin territory, they participated in government, became lead miners, farmers, bankers, fishers, printers, and opened their own shops, breweries, and leather tanning businesses.

When many European immigrants first came to the Wisconsin territory, they did not have enough money to buy land. They had to work to earn money before they could buy land, even though it was only $1.25 an acre. European American women could own property only if they remained single. Once they married, their property became their husband's property.

During the territorial days, neighbors helped one another. They worked together to build cabins and barns. They helped each other clear land, plow, plant, and harvest crops. People also shared tools since few tools were available. People began organizing churches. Church groups also organized their own schools.

FIGURE 4–2 Original text for student discussion about their family's perspective on life in the Wisconsin Territory

decided what they liked and disliked about being part of the North-west Territory and the Wisconsin Territory. This strategy followed the recommended best teaching practices in social studies education:

- Explore a variety of cultures.

- Involve students in inquiry and problem solving.

- Form mixed ability groups and have students participate in inter-active and cooperative study processes.[10]

Each of the six families had a unique identity. The Menominee family, one of the indigenous nations, wanted to remain in Wisconsin, their homeland, despite efforts by the U.S. government to move them to Minnesota. Another indigenous nation, the Ho-Chunk family, also desired to remain in their homeland of Wisconsin, but the U.S. government pressured them to move to a reservation in Iowa. The English mining family was very poor, lived with relatives until they could build their own cabin, and was supported by the father's lead mining and older children's employment by neighboring families. The wealthy German American family owned five hundred acres of farmland and employed several hired girls and hired hands to work for them. The young German couple had recently immigrated from Germany. They lived with and worked for a German American farmer until they earned enough money to send for their children remaining in Germany, buy farmland, and build their own cabin. The Yankee family moved to the region from New York and now owned 150 acres of land for their new home.

After the students talked within their own families about what they liked and disliked about being part of the Northwest Territory and the Wisconsin Territory, we summarized each family's ideas on a large chart during a whole class discussion. Students wrote individual journal entries giving their views on how their family felt about being part of each territory and worked with their family members to dramatize or illustrate in drawings their family's lifestyle during the Wisconsin Territory era.

In addition to the dramatizations by the Menominee and wealthy German American family described earlier, the remaining families also created drawings or dramatizations illustrating their lives in Wisconsin before statehood. Two members of the Ho-Chunk family created a drawing in which they illustrated an imaginary meeting they had with the U.S. president asking if they could have freedom and vote, but the president refused. Charlotte and Denise, two additional members of the Ho-Chunk family, dramatized life before and after Europeans.

Charlotte held up a large sheet of green paper and said, "This is our land before. What a nice day for gathering." She picked several ears of corn and handed them to Denise who put them in a basket. Then Charlotte explained, "Okay, our day of gathering is over." When Charlotte held up a very small sheet of green paper, Denise announced, "Wow, our land is sure getting smaller." Charlotte concurred, "Yeah, this is our land after some Europeans started moving in." During the next scene, Charlotte represented a U.S. governmental official and asked, "Could you move now?" Denise, representing the Ho-Chunk, protested, "But, we've been here all our lives! Why do we have to move now?" Charlotte clarified, "Because we're going to move here." Denise complained, "But that's not fair!" and walked away. Charlotte and Denise switched roles for the next scene. Charlotte, a Ho-Chunk, asked Denise, a governmental official, "May I run for leader?" Denise quickly refused, "You may not, we're the only people who can run for leaders. You won't do any good here." The final scene took place several months later when Charlotte asked again, "May I vote?" Denise again refused, "No, you may not. We're the only people who can vote. Why don't you go and not come back?" Then Denise concluded, "The Ho-Chunk people were forced to live on a reservation."

The Yankee family drew a large picture to illustrate their movement from New York to Wisconsin during the territorial days. They drew pictures of buying land, building log cabins, barns, and churches, and farming. They also depicted people building roads, one of the changes the government was making in the Wisconsin Territory. The German immigrant family drew a picture of someone plowing in a field, the German American farmer who was allowing them to live with and work for him, and the farmer's house. Next to an illustration of the German immigrant couple, their hopes for the future were written, "I hope we can send for our children soon." The English mining family illustrated their lifestyle with several miners, buckets to hold the lead they mined, and small cabins for their homes. They also included another farmhouse where family members who did not mine worked in order to help support their family.

When we interviewed students at the end of the unit, we discovered that most learned one main idea about what their family's life might have been like when Wisconsin was part of the Northwest Territory. The Menominee family members did not like the government's efforts to take their land and the European Americans' movement onto their lands. In contrast, the Ho-Chunk family liked having the land more to themselves, which allowed them to meet their needs and practice traditions. The English mining family lamented how hard everyone in the family had to work while the young German immigrant couple complained about having to live with someone else and not having their own land, but liked the low taxes. The wealthy German American family appreciated having a great deal of land, but was concerned about keeping Native Americans off "their" land. The Yankee family liked the religious freedom and availability of land for farming, but worried about crowded conditions as more people moved into the territory.

When the fourth graders were questioned during individual interviews about their family's situation as Wisconsin became a separate territory, most demonstrated an understanding of significant aspects of their family's lives at that time. The Menominee family continued to complain about government efforts to take their land for Europeans and disliked their lack of voting rights and opportunities to be governmental leaders even though they owned the land necessary for both rights. Susan, part of the Menominee family, explained:

> More and more Europeans kept on coming over and taking more of our land. We couldn't vote when there was an election. The only way we could vote was to be civilized. They were trying to force us off the land because they needed the land for Europeans.[11]

The Ho-Chunk family also lamented the European movement onto their lands and efforts to move them to a different state. They preferred to remain in the Wisconsin Territory. Jim, a Ho-Chunk family member, elaborated:

> We liked that we could live there. We didn't want to leave. We didn't want Wisconsin to become a state because then we might lose some of our land. We need all the land. If we lose some land, we could lose some people too because we wouldn't have much land. We didn't worry about the new laws they were starting to come out with. We could be free. We just wanted to live in Wisconsin Territory so we wouldn't have to go anywhere else.[12]

The English mining family complained about the taxes they had to pay while living in the Wisconsin Territory and their lack of voting rights because they did not own land. Chia, a member of this family, expressed her concern with her family's economic struggles:

> We liked that they let us go mining, but disliked that everybody in the family has to go to work [to support the family]. We couldn't vote. If it became a state, we would have to pay taxes, and we don't have enough money. Women couldn't vote.[13]

Similarly, the young German immigrant couple protested the taxes because of their limited income and their need to use money to build a house. Maria elaborated on her family's economic problems:

> We didn't like that we had to live with a farmer [and not have our own house]. We liked that we had a house [place to live]. We could farm. We could get money and send it to the kids in Germany and Europe. We didn't like that we had to pay taxes. We didn't want to pay taxes because we didn't have that much money to support the government.[14]

During the end-of-the-unit interviews, we hoped every member of the wealthy German American family understood that they could afford to pay the taxes and were eligible to become a government leader. Patty clearly explained her family's perspective.

> We couldn't really keep the Native Americans off the land. They may still be on land that we wanted. We liked it because we could go off our land and have plenty of room to go everywhere. We had to pay more taxes. My family liked it better because we could afford the taxes. We could become a government leader.[15]

Rameen, one member of the Yankee family, knew his family could build farms because of more land available in the Wisconsin Territory than in New York, which was the primary motivation for moving to the new territory.

> We liked that we were building roads and working jobs. We disliked that people were moving in and out and it would be crowded. It felt weird because we were the only ones who could vote. We thought that usually everyone could vote. We liked that there was lots of territory that you could buy. We could build lots of farms. It was better than where we were before. There was more land to buy.[16]

FOCUS ON YOUR STATE:
LIFE BEFORE STATEHOOD

In order to offer opportunities for your students to explore the experiences of different groups living in the colony or territory which eventually became your state, you might:

• Identify the main cultural groups and their socioeconomic levels for residents of your colony or territory prior to statehood by contacting the state historical society. Include Native American nations as well as immigrant groups from different countries and states.

• Solicit resources (books and other print documents, photographs, videos, websites, and guest speakers) from the state and local historical societies and Native American nations about the lifestyles of different groups prior to statehood, the type of government which existed prior to statehood, and who participated in the early government.

• Locate resources on the governmental structure of the Native nations living in your territory and invite students to compare that structure with the new European American government of your territory. They might compare who could participate and how leaders were chosen. For an introduction to Native American governments, see "Native American Governments in Today's Curriculum" and *How to Teach About American Indians.*[17]

• Organize the resources for your students to complete research on each of the main cultural groups. They might investigate such questions: What natural resources enabled Native people to live successfully in your colony or territory? What natural and cultural resources attracted immigrant groups to your area? How did each group provide for their basic necessities? How successful was each group in meeting basic needs? What might each cultural group like about living in your colony or territory? What might they dislike? How might they feel about more European and European American immigrants moving into the territory? What type of government existed in your colony or territory prior to statehood? What were the criteria for becoming governmental leaders? Who were the governmental leaders? Which culture and gender did these leaders belong to? Which groups had the right to participate in the colonial or territorial government through voting? What rights did each cultural group have in the colony or territory? For an overview of rights for residents of the Northwest Territory, students might read "The Best System We Could Get."[18]

• Offer opportunities for students to present their research on their groups' lifestyle and participation in the government prior to statehood. Students might also address the fairness of who had a voice in government before becoming a state.

CONFLICTS IN VIEWS ABOUT BECOMING A STATE: CONSTRUCTING ARGUMENTS

In this portion of the unit, we asked students to question if Wisconsin should become a state. For this focus, we continued to address the Power, Authority, and Governance and Civic Ideals and Practices strands of the national, state, and local standards. We also included the multicultural emphasis on integrating different cultural group's experiences and perspectives and raising the issues of sexism, racism, and classism. The fourth graders were encouraged to consider who benefited if Wisconsin no longer remained a territory but became a separate state. We wanted students to understand the government's requirements for a territory to become a state, the effects on their family if the territory became a state, who had voting rights to determine if the territory became a state, and the fairness of these rights.

Students continued to work in their family groups to consider the effects on their family if the territory became a state. They were asked to choose roles, although we clarified that girls did not have to become mothers and boys did not have to assume the father role. After much discussion, the Menominee and Ho-Chunk families decided who would serve as an elder, mother, father, and child in each family. The German immigrant family chose the roles of mother, father, and the German American farmer the family lived with. The wealthy German American family and poor English mining families arrived at the role of mother, father, and child. Because we could not find appropriate reading materials for the fourth graders, we created our own based on our research.[19] A copy is shown in Figure 4–3. As a family, the students read and discussed our original summaries of the conditions necessary for Wisconsin to become a state and different views in favor of and against Wisconsin's transition to statehood. After considering within their families the assorted views on Wisconsin changing to a state or remaining a territory, students individually recorded their decision. By observing these small group discussions, we noticed that students offered very diverse perspectives regarding statehood within their own families and could not reach a consensus on the final decision.

The Ho-Chunk family, consisting of Charlotte, Jim, Denise, and Jacob, argued at length about Wisconsin becoming a state. After completing the reading, most did not believe Ho-Chunk people would benefit from statehood.

Jacob: (Reading aloud from the sheet) Does your family believe Wisconsin should become a state?

Denise: I don't think it should become a state because . . .

Charlotte: More Europeans come in and we couldn't vote. If it's a separate state, we wouldn't be able to vote for the leaders and stuff. I don't think it should become a separate state.

Jim: I think if we became a state, it would be easier to know where you are instead of being in some unknown territory that you don't

SHOULD WISCONSIN BECOME A STATE IN 1846–1848?

Name _____ Date _____

1. List your family's cultural background, the names of the family members, and their roles:

_____

_____

_____

_____

2. How could Wisconsin become a state?

First, in order for Wisconsin to change from a territory to a state, there had to be sixty thousand voters living in the Wisconsin Territory. Voters were free men, at least twenty-one years old, who owned land, and had lived in the area for two years. Second, the Territorial Governor asked the voters to vote on whether or not they wanted the Wisconsin Territory to become a state.

Third, if the voters decided they wanted Wisconsin to become a state, then the Territorial Governor asked a group of people to hold a meeting or a convention. At this meeting they wrote the laws or constitution for the new state of Wisconsin. All people living in the new state had to obey these laws.

Fourth, after the constitution or laws were written, the voters had to vote to agree with these laws. Finally, if the voters agreed these were good laws to have in Wisconsin, the Territorial Governor asked the United States Congress to make Wisconsin a state.

3. Should Wisconsin become a state?

Read the next part and discuss with your family whether or not Wisconsin should become a state. Think about how your family would benefit and how your family might be harmed if Wisconsin became a state.

Some people believed the Wisconsin Territory should not become a state. Those immigrants who had been living in the territory longer than others did not want any more demands from the government.

(continues)

They wanted to be left alone. They did not want to pay taxes to the United States government if Wisconsin became a part of the United States. They already had to pay some taxes to help the territorial government and their local government work.

Some people also thought Wisconsin should not become a state because many new immigrants from Europe could not speak English. They would not understand enough to vote. Some people were not sure whom to trust as good leaders if Wisconsin became a state. They did not know whom to vote for when they chose governmental leaders.

For Native people living in Wisconsin, becoming a state meant even more European Americans would move into the area. Most Native people were not allowed to vote or be part of the government when Wisconsin was a territory or state.

Some people wanted Wisconsin to become a state. Those European American immigrants who had recently moved into Wisconsin wanted to elect their state leaders. They wanted to become part of the United States and vote for president and vice president. They also believed that if Wisconsin became a state, more European Americans or Yankees and European immigrants would move into Wisconsin.

Discuss with your family: Does your family believe Wisconsin should become a state? Why?

4. **Who in your family could vote to decide if Wisconsin should become a state?**

5. **Discuss with your family: Do you think this is fair? Why or why not?**

6. **Did Wisconsin become a state?**
   By 1846 enough European and European American or Yankee immigrants eligible to vote were living in Wisconsin. They voted in favor of Wisconsin becoming a state. Henry Dodge, the Territorial Governor, asked for men or delegates to meet as a convention to decide on the constitution or laws.

   Delegates were chosen to attend this meeting. They wrote the first constitution or laws in 1846. This constitution allowed married women to have the right to own property. Usually women could own and control property only when they were single. When women got married, their husbands owned their property and controlled it.

   This constitution also outlawed banks because the first banks in the Wisconsin Territory went out of business and people lost their savings. People did not trust banks. The delegates discussed giving African American men the right to vote and hold offices in the state government. However, they decided not to put it in the constitution. Instead, they wrote it as a separate ballot. Voters could decide if they wanted African American men to have the right to vote.

When the voters, who were all men, voted on this first constitution or set of laws, they voted no. They did not believe married women should have the right to own and control their own property. Voters believed this would harm marriages. Many voters did not think women should engage in public activities with their property. Women should remain at home. Voters did not agree that there should be no banks in Wisconsin. Voters also voted against African American men having the right to vote on a separate ballot.

In 1848 Territorial Governor Dodge called for a second convention or meeting to write another constitution the voters would like. Most of the delegates to this convention were different from the delegates to the first convention. The delegates took out the part of the first constitution which said that married women could own property and the section which outlawed banks in Wisconsin.

The voters voted to agree with the new constitution. On May 29, 1848, Wisconsin became a state. It was the 30th state in the United States.

7. **Discuss with your family: Who do you think should have the right to vote after Wisconsin became a state? Why?**

8. **Who had the right to vote after Wisconsin became a state?**
   European American or White men at least twenty-one years old had the right to vote in Wisconsin when it became a state. Some Native men were given the right to vote. Oneida men were given the right to vote after they moved to Wisconsin in the 1830s. The only other Native men who could vote were those considered "civilized." That meant they had adopted European American ways of life and lived apart from their nation. Most Native men could not vote in state or national elections when Wisconsin became a state. No African American men or women of any culture could vote after Wisconsin became a state.

9. **Discuss with your family: Do you think who had the right to vote was fair? Why or why not?**

FIGURE 4–3 Original summary for student discussion about becoming a state

know what it is. You'd never know where you were. I'm somewhere in the Northwest Territory.

Charlotte: But if Wisconsin becomes a state, that means more Europeans are gonna come and we won't be able to pick our leaders and what we feel.

Jim: We still can't pick our leaders [in the Northwest or Wisconsin Territory].

Charlotte: We don't get to share our opinions, what we want for the government and our leaders and stuff.

The Yankee family, Rameen, Kay, and Mandy, were also divided about the transition to statehood. The family already owned land and the father, played by Mandy, was eligible to vote for statehood. However, they considered many factors in favor of and against statehood.

Rameen: I think Wisconsin should become a state because we already have land, so we have somewhere to live.

Kay: And food to eat and clothes on our back.

Mandy: I don't think we should become a state for the same reason it says here [on the sheet]. I don't think we should have any demands from the government. I don't think we should have to pay taxes.

Kay: I think Wisconsin should become a state because we need more jobs. They put clothes on our back and food on the table.

Rameen: We have farmland. We can grow crops. We should stay here. It won't really affect us.

Mandy: I think it would. More people would be moving in and we could be spending our money on other things like Kay was saying, like food and stuff.

Rameen: But if people move in, they couldn't go on our territory.

Mandy: Yeah, I know, but we would pay taxes.

Kay: How are you gonna get food if you don't work and get money?

Rameen: If Wisconsin government doesn't become a state, we would still have to pay taxes.

Mandy: Yeah, I know, but not as much, not as much as if Wisconsin did become a state.

Rameen: When Wisconsin becomes a state, we'll have more land, the government is going to make the Indians live on reservations so there would be more land.

Mandy: It will get crowded, there'd be so many people. They'd take more trees, use trees for their firewood and kill more animals and things for food.

During individual interviews at the end of the unit, all students could explain some of the main conditions necessary for Wisconsin to change from a territory to a state: (1) the presence of sixty thousand voters or free men who were at least twenty-one years old, owned land, and lived in the area two years; (2) voters' agreement that the Wisconsin Territory should become a state; (3) a new constitution approved by voters; and (4) action from U.S. Congress to make Wisconsin a state.

Most students articulated their family's perspective on Wisconsin becoming a state during the interviews. The Menominee and Ho-Chunk families did not want Wisconsin to become a state because more Europeans might move into the region and force Native people off their land and onto reservations. Students explained that Native people did not have a vote, could not participate in the government, and did not want to pay taxes. Jacob clarified a Ho-Chunk view:

> We didn't like it because we didn't even get to say anything about it. We didn't want it to become a state. We wanted it to remain part of the Northwest Territory. As soon as it became a state, Europeans would notice it more. They also would have kicked us out and put us on these little reservations.[20]

Most members of the English mining family could explain during individual interviews that they did not want Wisconsin to become a state because they would have to pay taxes. In Jake's words, the taxes would be "Way too much."[21] The young German immigrant couple also did not want Wisconsin to become a state because of the greater taxes when they needed money to buy land and build a house. Neal clarified his family's perspective: "We really didn't want

Wisconsin to become a state. They needed the money to build their houses and to build farms and maybe to buy land to plant stuff."[22]

During the interviews, most members of the wealthy German American family recognized they wanted Wisconsin to become a state because they could pay taxes, become governmental leaders, and move Native Americans off their land more easily. Patty elaborated on her family's point of view regarding statehood:

> Our family thought it should become a state because we could pay taxes and become a government leader. Not to be rude or anything, but we could kick Native Americans off our land easily. More people would own land closer together so it would be a little safer. They could also speak English.[23]

Most members of the Yankee family during the interviews demonstrated an understanding of benefits for their family if Wisconsin became a state. They could purchase more land to grow additional crops for income and food, and they were eligible to vote. However, Mandy, the Yankee family member who did not want Wisconsin to become a state, offered defensible reasons about how her family would not benefit from statehood:

> Most of our group thought Wisconsin should become a state and I thought it should not. I thought it would be too crowded and then we wouldn't have as much trees left because of chopping them down. You would have to pay lots of taxes and there would be lots of regulations. Kay kept saying, "Where are we going to live and get clothes and food?" I was saying we can hunt for our food. The Indians got along that way, there is nothing wrong with living that way, so why not live that way?[24]

Voting for Statehood

In order to illustrate the significant effects of voting rights on the decision to make Wisconsin a state, we organized a voting simulation. We posed the question to the class, "Should Wisconsin become a state?" During the first vote, we explained that all adults in each family were eligible to vote and distributed ballots to them, including the Menominee, Ho-Chunk, English mining family, and young German immigrant couple. From our earlier readings and discussions, these families, for the most part, did not want Wisconsin to become a state (approximately fifteen of the twenty class members). Not surprising, the outcome of the first vote was that Wisconsin remained a territory.

For the second vote, we clarified that only those who met all the criteria were eligible to vote: (1) males at least twenty-one years old; (2) owned land; and (3) lived in the area at least two years. The qualified voters were then reduced to three: the Yankee family's father (played by Mandy who had argued against statehood earlier), the wealthy German American family's father (played by Hua), and the German farmer (played by Carlos) with whom the young German immigrant couple were living. We distributed a ballot to each student who portrayed one of these three roles. Before we counted the ballots, we asked the class to speculate on what the outcome would be. Patty thoughtfully responded, "I think it would become a state because all the people who voted no can't vote now." To our surprise, when we counted the ballots, the outcome was two to one against Wisconsin becoming a state. The Ho-Chunk and Menominee families immediately began cheering and pounding their desks while the German immigrant couple smiled broadly. In contrast, Patty, from the wealthy German American family, opened her mouth widely in surprise and disbelief at the outcome. Two members of the Yankee family slumped in their desks in disagreement with the vote.

We wondered why not all the qualified voters followed the majority of their family members' perspective as we expected. Perhaps students were persuaded by arguments from others about significant negative consequences, especially for the Ho-Chunk and Menominee, if Wisconsin became a state. Only a few students spoke about the unexpected outcome of the second vote:

> When Native Americans voted, there was more who voted. The vote was more no's than yes's because there were more Native Americans than European Americans. When we took the Native Americans' voting privileges away, more of the votes were toward Wisconsin becoming a state. Somehow the no's still won. I expected that once we took the Native American privileges away, that the vote would turn out yes, Wisconsin should become a state, just like it did in 1848. It turned out that Wisconsin didn't become a state in our little skit.[25]

During the interviews at the unit's close, several students understood the unfairness of so few people having the right to vote during our second election, when we followed the governmental regulations of who had voting rights. Carlos complained about the limited voting rights, although he was eligible to vote in both elections as the German farmer who shared his home with the German immigrant couple:

> There was only a few people that could vote. It wasn't fair. If you didn't own land, then you couldn't vote, or pick the leaders. They can make laws that you have to leave the land. Then they can stay in office. I didn't think that was fair.[26]

FOCUS ON YOUR STATE: DIFFERENT PERSPECTIVES ON STATEHOOD

As you and your students study your state's transition to statehood, you might investigate the conditions necessary for your colony or territory to become a state and how the main cultural groups viewed the change to statehood. You could:

• Contact local and state historical societies for resources on the criteria for becoming a state, the qualifications for the right to vote for statehood, which cultural and gender groups had a voice in voting for statehood, the benefits and drawbacks of becoming a state for residents, and different cultural groups' perspectives on statehood.

• Contact Native American nations or your state historical society for resources on how Native people who resided in your area prior to statehood viewed the change to statehood.

• Ask your students to investigate how different cultural groups might benefit or suffer from the transition to statehood, the fairness of the criteria for voting rights, and which cultural and gender groups could vote for statehood. For a good introduction on reasons for limiting voting rights to male property owners, your students might read "Elections in the Colonies."[27]

• Prepare a voting simulation allowing adult members of all cultural groups in your colony or territory to participate in the vote for statehood, and then prepare another simulation limiting the voting rights to only those adult cultural group members who meet the criteria for voting. Compare the outcomes of the two votes and discuss reasons for the outcomes.

VOTING RIGHTS : CRITICAL LITERACY AND DIVERSE VIEWS

Our focus on groups given voting rights after statehood and national and state activists who struggled to obtain voting rights for disenfranchised groups allowed us to continue to address the national thematic strands of the Power, Authority, and Governance and Civic Ideals and Practices and the corresponding state and local social studies standards. Through the inclusion of the Power, Authority, and Governance thematic strand, we provided opportunities for the fourth graders to examine how the new state government met the needs and wants of some groups to have a voice in their government but not others, dealt with conflicts between different groups over voting rights, and demonstrated such concepts as fairness, equity, and justice in laws determining criteria for participation in the new state government.[28] By addressing the sexism and racism inherent in the criteria for voting rights, we were also integrating the multicultural education emphasis on integrating different cultural group's experiences and perspectives and raising such issues as sexism and racism in the social studies curriculum.[29]

The Civic Ideals and Practices thematic strand was also important in this part of the state history unit as the students had opportunities to learn about the actions people took to influence such public policies as the denial of voting rights to women of all groups, African Americans, and some Native Americans. In addition, we hoped the fourth graders would understand how citizen action to extend voting rights can strengthen the "common good" or the participation of diverse groups in state and national government.[30] The Civic Ideals and

Practices thematic strand was very similar to the multicultural education emphasis on social action or helping students learn about actions they and others can take to reduce inequalities in the world around them.[31] By introducing the fourth graders to voting rights activists within the state and the country, we hoped the students would learn how they, too, could influence public policies to allow many people's participation in government. These ideas were also part of the state and local Political Science and Citizenship standard:

• Students will explain how various forms of civic action such as running for political office, voting, signing an initiative, and speaking at a hearing can contribute to the well-being of the community.[32]

Literacy and Critical Literacy

By asking students to construct meaning from our original summary and published texts regarding the events that led to Wisconsin becoming a state, who had the right to vote after statehood, and activists who struggled for voting rights, we incorporated several school district literacy objectives. We provided opportunities for the fourth graders to:

• Demonstrate an understanding of a piece of literature.

• Express and support an opinion on the author's purpose.

• Evaluate the behavior of characters from different cultural perspectives.

• Paraphrase informational and expository text.

Critical literacy was also part of our unit through our introduction of published and original texts which overtly addressed issues of inequality, especially political inequality, and leaders who fought against unequal rights for women and African Americans.[33] We encouraged students to analyze readings for the fairness of who should have the right to vote after Wisconsin became a state, who actually enjoyed this right, reasons people fought for racial and gender equality, and why others opposed granting equal rights to women and

African Americans. Through discussions and writing, students were invited to make personal connections with the abolitionists and suffragists in our readings and empathize with their experiences.[34]

Who Should Have the Right to Vote?
Family Critical Readings and Discussions

We asked each family group to cooperatively finish reading and discuss the original summary "Should Wisconsin Become a State in 1846–1848?" (Figure 4–3) which briefly described the events leading to statehood and who had the right to vote after statehood. We listed the criteria for voting rights, including: males; from European American, Oneida, or civilized Native American cultural backgrounds; and at least twenty-one years of age. Students were invited to analyze the justice of these criteria. We encouraged the fourth graders to consider different perspectives on who had the right to vote in Wisconsin, including women's and men's views from Menominee and Ho-Chunk nations, poor English mining and German immigrant families, Yankee land-owning families, and wealthy German American immigrant families. After they completed the reading, students discussed within their families who should have the right to vote after Wisconsin became a state and the fairness of who enjoyed voting rights.

During their small group discussion, most members of the Menominee family complained about their lack of voting rights. Xee began, "We would have to live away from our tribe to vote, that wouldn't be fair." John added, "We should be able to vote without leaving our tribe. I think it's not fair." Then Susan joined in with a different view about the opportunity to vote, even if it meant becoming "civilized:" "Because Native people could vote then instead of sitting there and watching more and more Europeans coming. They could have part of it, too. It's fair. They can vote instead of just letting European American men vote, so they can take part of it." She quoted the reading, "Only Native men who could vote were those considered civilized." John clarified, "You have to be like Europeans, you couldn't be part of the tribe." However, Susan countered, "You could still be part of the tribe, still have powwows." John disagreed, "No, it was 'civilized,' I think it's not fair because we can't vote, unless we have to be like them. We should just vote however we want. We own over fifty acres of land and lived here over two years."

During individual interviews with students at the end of the unit, we discovered that most students developed a clear understanding of who had the right to vote in Wisconsin after it became a state. They clarified that certain groups of men over twenty-one years of age could vote, including European American men, Oneida men (given voting rights when they moved to a reservation in Wisconsin in the 1820s), and Native American men considered civilized. Several students accurately explained "civilized" as meaning those Native men who had given up traditional ways of life, no longer lived with their nation or tribe, and adopted a European American lifestyle. Charlotte, who assumed the role of a Ho-Chunk family member during this unit, complained about the need for Native people to be considered civilized in order to vote:

> "Civilized" means they were doing the ways of the Europeans. Instead of wearing the deerskins they wore, they would wear cloth. They would adjust to the ways of the Europeans. That wasn't fair. Any Indian that lived in Wisconsin should be able to vote that is over twenty-one. They should have the same rules as the White men. They should still be able to vote even if they are not "civilized." Everybody is different. They can't always be like other people.[35]

Many students also spoke of the unfairness of who was eligible to vote at this time and thought everyone who was twenty-one years old and a citizen should be able to vote. In the role of the mother in the wealthy German American family whose father could vote, Patty still believed the limited people who could vote for their leaders was unfair:

> After Wisconsin became a state, European men and Oneida men and Anishinabe [Native American] that were considered civilized could vote. No African Americans could vote. It wasn't fair because they are people too and they have the right. It will be their leader too. Why shouldn't they be able to vote? They have to live with this person and what if I don't even want this person.[36]

Rameen, who assumed the role of a Yankee land-owning family member, agreed that more people besides European American men were qualified to vote. "I thought it wasn't fair because women and African Americans are as smart as men and Oneida. I think they should have the right to vote."[37]

National Voting Rights Activists:
Elizabeth Cady Stanton and Susan B. Anthony

The same year that Wisconsin became a state (1848), the first Women's Rights Convention was held in Seneca Falls, New York. We wanted students to be aware that the controversy over voting rights existed at the state and national levels. In order to help the fourth graders learn about national leaders who worked to abolish slavery and obtain voting rights for women and African Americans from 1848–1900, such as Elizabeth Cady Stanton, Susan B. Anthony, Sojourner Truth, and Frederick Douglass, we used published texts and original choral readings and expository readings about these four notable people. We first read aloud the picture book, *The Ballot Box Battle*,[38] to the class. It introduced students to Elizabeth Cady Stanton's childhood struggles to prove to her father that girls were equal to boys and her efforts as an adult to help women gain the right to vote. The fourth graders were encouraged throughout the reading to discuss different meanings and interpretations of the text.

At the end of the reading, I asked the students why they thought the author wrote the text. After discussing possible ideas within their small groups, Mandy explained, "Her ancestors had the problem that they couldn't vote. They were women and they wanted to vote." Judy added, "The author wanted to show that women and girls are the same as boys." Maria agreed and Susan elaborated, "To show that girls are qualified in most of the things boys do." Next Charlotte contributed, "She was trying to prove this was hard for women when this happened, to vote and stuff." Jacob affirmed this view with, "I think the author wrote the book because she wanted to tell about one of the women who tried to fight for the freedom to vote." Extending the discussion still further, Denise explained, "To show the self-determination women had before they had the right to vote."

Following this reading and discussion, we distributed the expository booklet "Failure Is Impossible"[39] to each family group to encourage students to learn about Susan B. Anthony's efforts to achieve equality for women and African Americans. Students decided how they would read the booklet, then discussed why Anthony wanted to abolish slavery and have equality for women, what experiences helped her recognize women were not treated fairly, what changes Anthony and Elizabeth Cady Stanton wanted to make, and the factors encouraging Anthony to work for so many years to gain voting rights for women. Following each family discussion, we summarized important ideas as a class. Several students spoke about the injustices of slavery, which likely motivated Anthony to abolish it. They also raised the issue of Anthony being paid only half of what men earned in teaching and being expected to give her money to her father rather than keep it for herself during the nineteenth century.

Jim: It wasn't fair for people to have to be slaves and have their family sold as slaves. Susan B. Anthony wanted everybody to be equal to each other.

Maria: People might die.

Ava: Who are you talking about?

Maria: Slaves.

Susan: Susan B. Anthony was against slavery because they were being used just for working. They didn't get no pay.

Neal: She was against slavery so families wouldn't get split up. (We elaborated on Neal's idea.)

Carlos: Most of the time slaves were bought, a person owned them and would be mean to them working.

Denise: Because of what happened to her in her past jobs, when she wanted to be a teacher and she said she'd only get half-pay. (We asked the class to elaborate on this idea.)

Jake: Women would get half of what the man made. Maybe they thought women wouldn't do that good a job teaching.

Jacob: Because they thought women weren't as smart, so they couldn't do as good a job.

Rameen: Because they thought men, people who could vote, might be able to get more pay.

Mandy: Maybe people thought men had more experience because they could do more things than girls or women could.

Xee: People don't think men and women should be paid equally.

Charlotte: Maybe men were more smarter and educated because they went to school when they were little. And girls and women had to stay home and learn how to cook and clean and stuff instead of going and learning.

Carlos: Girls had to dress in white dresses and play with dolls and boys could go outside and explore.

Charlotte: When she took the teaching job, she had to give the money to her father and stuff. (Thelma elaborated on this idea by citing her experiences of giving her earnings to her family when she was growing up.)

Students then wrote letters to either Elizabeth Cady Stanton or Susan B. Anthony explaining their views on the importance of these women's work. The letters captured important elements of Stanton's and Anthony's struggles to gain equality for women, students' feelings about the value of the women's accomplishments, and descriptions of benefits they or their family members received from Stanton's and Anthony's achievements.

Dear Susan B. Anthony,

I think it's good that you fought for the chance for women to vote and what you belived in. I also think it's good that you wouldn't pay the fine when you put the ballot in the ballot box. I feel glad that you stood up for what you believe in. I also feel that it wasn't fair that when you were a child that girls were expected to play with dolls and be perfect little angels when boys could go out and explore. I feel that it's important that you fought for the chance for women to vote.

Sincerely, Patty

Dear Susan B. Anthony,

I feel sorry for you because you couldn't vote, keep your money or work at any job you wanted. You proved that women are as good as any man. You make people feel proud for who they really are. If it weren't for you and Liz, women wouldn't have hardly any JUSTICE!!! I feel good because now everyone can vote.

> Gratefully, Mandy
> P.S. Thanks a lot!

Dear Susan B. Anthony,

I feel like you did the right thing for this nation. You should be proud of what you have done. You encouraged a lot of women. Even though I'm a boy I think women should vote.

> Sincerely, Jake

Dear Susan B. Anthony,

You were very brave to go against the law just so women could vote. You were right when they made you pay $100.00 just because you tried to vote. And a question for you, what made you stand up for all the women? And why were you the, well, the only woman to stand up to the judge? And another thing, it's like you made your own law and you don't work for the U.S. government. If you would not have done that, women would not be voting. Even though I am a boy, I think girls should have the right to vote. You must be very proud. And now you will probably be in the history book. You were just as important as George Washington and anybody else.

> Sincerely, Danny

Dear Elizabeth Cady Stanton,

You did the right thing to stand up and say that women have the right to vote. You and Susan B. Anthony made good choices. You did a great job for standing up to the men and saying the right stuff. Susan B. Anthony and you changed a lot of bad stuff to good stuff like: slavery, money rights, working rights, property rights, education rights, speaking rights, and suffrage or voting rights. I feel glad that the laws were changed because if it was not changed women would not get to vote. Elizabeth Cady Stanton, you did a wonderful job with Susan B. Anthony. You and Susan B. Anthony make a great team.

> Sincerely, Hua

Dear Elizabeth Cady Stanton,

You proved to people all over that women are just as good as men. You also fought for the women's right to vote. You fought for a lot of things and after you died a lot of the things you fought against were changed to how you would have liked them. I thought that you were very brave to stand up for what you believed in. I think that you should feel very proud of yourself because you changed a lot of bad things to good things. Thank you very much for being so very brave and standing up for what you believed in. Thank you.

Sincerely, Charlotte

During individual end-of-the-unit interviews, most students articulated some of Elizabeth Cady Stanton's and Susan B. Anthony's goals in working for equality. They knew Stanton and Anthony wanted to: work for equal rights; show women were as good as men; end slavery; win voting rights for women and African Americans; gain property rights or the rights of women to keep their property when they married and keep the money they earned; achieve the right for women and girls to go to school; realize the right for women to have different jobs and earn the same as men; and secure the right for women to speak at meetings. Most fourth graders described Elizabeth Cady Stanton's activities to help women gain the right to vote. They explained she was very determined that women should have the right to vote and attempted to vote in an election, but was prevented from doing so by men at the polls. Several knew she made speeches in support of women's right to vote. Carlos seemed impressed with Stanton's courage for trying to vote when women were not allowed to exercise this constitutional right:

> Elizabeth Cady Stanton was very brave. She didn't care what other people thought about her going to vote, or at least try to vote. Even though she knew that she couldn't, she still went about every year if she could. She knew it wasn't fair that women couldn't vote. In the Constitution, any American citizen that is the legal limit of age could vote, but then the men said she couldn't vote.[40]

In addition, Neal recognized that sometimes women had to prove their worthiness in order to gain political equality:

> Women are just as good as any boy or man. Sometimes, people had to fight for their right to vote. Sometimes they had to prove that they could do what a boy or man could do. She [Stanton] really wanted to vote because she thought it was right.[41]

Most students learned that Susan B. Anthony worked for voting rights for women. Some students cited specific strategies she used to gain these rights, such as Anthony's attempt to vote in an election, her arrest and fine for this action, and her refusal to pay the fine. Patty was especially articulate in summarizing Anthony's and Stanton's struggles for women's suffrage:

> Susan B. Anthony got arrested for putting her voting ballot in the ballot box. She would not pay the fine. She thought that women were just as good as men. We should all be treated equally, so she thought, "I'm going to vote! I'm not going to pay the fine! You can take me to jail and I don't care!" They [Stanton and Anthony] wanted to change the rights for women because they practically didn't have any. They had to just go home because that was their place. They had to be perfect and obey everyone like they were some kind of animal.[42]

Several fourth graders also recognized Anthony's work to abolish slavery and gain voting rights for African Americans. Danny described his views on the injustice of slavery:

> She wanted to stop slavery because she didn't want White people to own Black people. The Black people didn't want to get sold. White people thought they were more important, so they would just sell them.[43]

National Voting Rights Activists:
Sojourner Truth and Frederick Douglass

Two additional activists who spoke out for equality for African Americans and women across the country during this same period were Sojourner Truth and Frederick Douglass. We led the class in an original choral reading highlighting aspects of Sojourner Truth's "Ain't I a Woman" speech, which she gave at the Women's Rights Convention in Ohio in 1851.[44] In our follow-up discussion, the class summarized that Sojourner Truth used words like "ain't" because she was born a slave and never had the opportunity to attend school. She cared about women's rights; had a strong belief in God; didn't like slavery because she "worked and worked and worked and never got anything in return"; didn't agree with ministers who said men were stronger; and she "had her own way of thinking."

We also read aloud a short summary of Frederick Douglass' life and work to end slavery and win equality for women and African Americans.[45] In order to provide additional background on Douglass before the reading, we explained that, like Sojourner Truth, Frederick Douglass was born a slave, but spoke out against slavery. We introduced other texts about Douglass and showed photographs and drawings of him at different times during his life.[46] When students questioned the time period when Truth and Douglass were living, we clarified they were adults at the same time as Anthony and Stanton (approximately 1850–1900). Following the reading, the class created a concept map of important ideas about Douglass' life:

disagreed with slavery

learned how to read and write

wrote a story about himself

had a clever escape [from slavery] plan

wanted equality

agreed with others who were fighting for equality

helped African American men first and helped women second [gain voting rights]

had practical ideas on change (help African American men first and women second)

became a hero.

Finally, the students produced a collage of drawings illustrating important ideas about Sojourner Truth and Frederick Douglass, shown in Figure 4–4.

During the interviews, most students understood the main purpose of Sojourner Truth's and Frederick Douglass' work, winning equality for African Americans and women. Students recognized that Sojourner Truth wanted to show that African Americans were equal

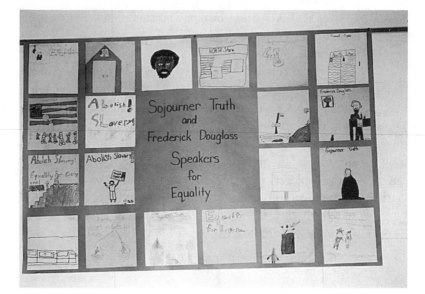

FIGURE 4–4 Class collage representing activists Sojourner Truth and Frederick Douglass

to European Americans and should have the right to vote and own property. She worked hard to win equality for African Americans and women and spoke out against and encouraged the abolishment of slavery. A few students defined Truth's main strategy for working for equality was through making speeches. Carlos acknowledged Truth's ability as a speaker and the messages she was trying to communicate to audiences about how women were treated and the cruelty of slavery:

> She [Truth] was a powerful speaker.[She said] when women needed help they were lifted in and out of carriages. They were to have the best everywhere. Nobody ever helps me to carriages, over mud puddles or gets me in any best places. Then she would say, "And ain't I a woman?" [She was trying to say] African American people didn't get help from White people. First she saw her children get stolen from slavery. She would cry, but nobody comforted her for that time. If it were the other way around, somebody would comfort a [European] American woman.[47]

Denise was concerned about the criticisms that clergymen made about women's efforts to gain equality, especially those directed at Sojourner Truth's speeches:

> Many people, especially men, did not want women to have the right to vote. She [Truth] was upset by that. Male ministers made fun of her speeches. She wasn't happy about that. They were ministers and she believes in God and now they turn on her. The ministers say that women have to be helped out of carriages and over mud puddles. She said, "Nobody ever helps me out of a carriage and ain't I a woman?" You can tell she never really had proper English because ain't isn't a word. [She was trying to say] she was as equal as any man. She could do the work and didn't need any help.[48]

Several students explained at least one of the tactics that Frederick Douglass used to gain voting rights for women and African Americans. One was through writing a book about his life as a slave and another was by giving speeches and publishing a newspaper, *The North Star*, encouraging equality and speaking against slavery. Several students described Douglass' approach of working first for voting rights for African American men and then focusing on gaining these rights for women. Carlos clarified Douglass' strategy to gain suffrage for these two groups:

> First he wanted African American men to get the right to vote. Then Elizabeth Cady Stanton and Susan B. Anthony were angry at him for doing that. I thought it was a smart idea to do it. If they asked for too many things at one time, they don't get anything. Frederick Douglass also had a newspaper called *The North Star*. He would write stuff about how women and African Americans should get the right to vote. Frederick Douglass was someone who tried to get equality for everyone.[49]

State Voting Rights Activists

In addition to introducing students to national activists for suffrage, we wanted students to learn that people in Wisconsin were also involved in gaining voting rights for women and African Americans. To provide diverse perspectives, we introduced students to groups who opposed the extension of voting rights to women and African

Americans. We found interesting texts on the suffrage movement in Wisconsin during the nineteenth and twentieth centuries written for adults, but nothing for elementary students.[50] In order to make this knowledge accessible for the students, we created an expository text, *Voting Rights for Women and African Americans in Wisconsin*, for the fourth graders to read and illustrate. A page of the text is shown in Figure 4–5. It described the many people, organizations, and strategies used to gain political equality for women and African Americans and different views in favor of and opposed to women's suffrage. Each student received one paragraph to read and illustrate to place in

When the delegates wrote the first constitution or set of laws for Wisconsin in 1846, they considered giving women and African Americans the right to vote. The voters voted against the first constitution which gave married women the right to own property after they married. They also voted against African Americans having the right to vote. Many people in Wisconsin were against slavery, but most did not want women and African Americans to have the right to vote.

FIGURE 4–5 A page from the class book *Voting Rights for Women and African Americans in Wisconsin*

a class book. We also encouraged students to study copies of photographs illustrating the different activities people engaged in as they worked for voting rights for women.[51] As the students read and illustrated their paragraph, several asked for help in pronouncing and understanding the meanings of words. After everyone finished illustrating their page, the students read their part of the class book aloud and explained their illustration. The remaining class members asked questions about the illustrations and we elaborated on the meaning of the text.

Despite the difficulty of some of the ideas and language, most students understood the main purpose of the original class book as showing how people worked for voting rights for women and African Americans in Wisconsin or why some groups did not want voting rights extended to these two groups. During individual interviews, a majority of students reported they learned the most from completing their illustration of the text. Jake succinctly explained European American men's resistance to voting rights for women and African Americans: "[European American] men were allowed to vote for a really long time. They voted continuously to not let African Americans and women vote."[52] Mandy also articulated her understanding of the reason for European American men's resistance to African Americans' and European American women's voting rights as "They would vote for the wrong things."[53] In addition, Neal understood that if women voted, marriages might be jeopardized:

> Men wanted women to stay home and that was the right thing for women to do. They took care of things at home. They thought [if women voted] it was going to ruin marriages. They [women] might vote for someone that they don't want to vote for and they might get into a fight.[54]

Finally, Tong understood that not all women were eager to vote. "Some women didn't want to vote, they weren't interested."[55]

Many fourth graders described at least one of the tactics people used to gain voting rights for women and African Americans. These included: creating organizations to discuss voting rights; holding meetings, parades, rallies, and conventions; riding in cars or boats to inform others about the importance of voting for women; giving speeches; publishing pamphlets explaining why women should vote; and discussing the value of voting rights with people at their homes. Charlotte summarized some of the strategies used to gain voting rights and why some opposed these rights:

> A lot of people fought for the women's right to vote after it was proved to them that women can be just as good as men. After women were able to prove to men that they were just as good as them, a lot of men took the side with them having the right to vote. A lot of women went in cars and on the streets, they marched with signs. They made speeches, [to] let people recognize that they needed a chance to vote, too. They go down the river in boats and hold up signs and shout to get the people's attention. They wouldn't let women vote because they thought they might shut down some of the different things that men enjoy doing, like maybe closing down liquor stores. They were afraid of that. They were worried too that if they let women vote, they would vote for the wrong people. If a woman ran for leader, then they might vote for the woman.[56]

FOCUS ON YOUR STATE: VOTING RIGHTS AND VOTING RIGHTS ACTIVISTS

In preparation for teaching about voting rights in your state following statehood, the qualifications for the right to vote, who had the right to vote and who did not, and activists in your state for political equality, you might:

• Contact your state historical society, Native American nations within your state, and local branches of such organizations as the League of Women Voters, National Organization for Women, and the National Organization for the Advancement of Colored People for resources on the criteria for voting rights immediately after statehood, who had the right to vote, and names of activists who fought for voting rights for disenfranchised people in your state. Guest speakers about state voting rights activists might especially be valuable for your students.

• Provide resources for your students to investigate who had voting rights following statehood, who did not, and why. The results of their research could be shared with the class.

• Form literature circles for your students to read and discuss texts about voting rights activists. If you are teaching in the West or Midwest, states which extended suffrage to women prior to the passage of the Nineteenth Amendment to the Constitution in 1919, your students might read several chapters from *The Day the Women Got the Vote: A Photo History of the Women's Rights Movement* and the state activist described in *When Esther Morris Headed West: Women, Wyoming, and the Right to Vote.*[57] For such national activists as Elizabeth Cady Stanton and Susan B. Anthony, your students could read: *They Shall Be Heard: Susan B. Anthony & Elizabeth Cady Stanton, Susan B. Anthony: And Justice for All,* or *You Want Women to Vote, Lizzie Stanton?*[58] To learn more about the activities of Sojourner Truth and Frederick Douglass, they might read: *Sojourner Truth: Ain't I a Woman, Walking the Road to Freedom: A Story About Sojourner Truth, A Picture Book of Sojourner Truth,* or *Escape from Slavery: The Boyhood of Frederick Douglass in His Own Words.*[59]

VOTING RIGHTS AND FAMILIES: MAKING CONNECTIONS BETWEEN GOVERNMENT AND OURSELVES

For the closing portion of our study on becoming a state and voting rights, we continued to address the Power, Authority, and Governance and Civic Ideals national thematic strands and the corresponding state and local social studies standards. We wanted the students to make personal connections between the importance of voting to have a voice in state and national government and their own families having a voice in government. We also wanted the students to discover that voting is both a right and responsibility of citizenship.[60] By asking students to interview an adult member of their family about voting, we hoped they would understand their families' views on the significance of political participation in government through voting.

By bringing out the students' families' diverse perspectives on voting and voting rights, we also integrated the multicultural education and best teaching practice emphasis on including different cultural group's perspectives and experiences, including the students themselves.[61]

Family Voting Interviews

We sent a letter to the families explaining the interview assignment and listed the questions their child should ask:

Are you eligible to vote? Why or why not?

Why do you think voting is important?

How would you feel if you could not vote?

Next, we modeled the interview process with Ava as the interviewer and Thelma as the interviewee. As Thelma responded to the questions, Ava recorded important words in Thelma's responses on the overhead projector so students could observe how they could record interview notes. Through this assignment, we hoped students would understand the current criteria for voting eligibility in Wisconsin and who in their family met these requirements. In addition, we wanted students to comprehend the importance of voting today by discovering how someone in their family viewed the significance of voting and their reaction to being denied the privilege to vote. After allowing a week for students to complete the assignment, we asked students to share the results of their interviews. We created a large chart summarizing the main ideas during our whole class discussion.

Most students completed the interview and were eager to report what they discovered to the class. When the fourth graders shared the results of the interviews, we discovered that several students had adult family members who were not U.S. citizens yet and could not vote. Rameen's family recently immigrated from India and his mother was a U.S. citizen and could vote, but not his father. Three Hmong students had family members who could not vote, including Chia's father and Xee's and Hua's mothers.

However, all students who shared their interviews spoke about the importance of voting to their family members. During our class discussion, Chia began with one reason why voting was important, "So we can have leaders," and was followed by Jim's contribution, "So we can get the people we want elected." Next Danny added, "It's kind of like that, but in a different way, that's how people elect their government representatives." Then Susan offered, "I want my voice to be heard." Patty elaborated, "By voting a person into office, the population that votes for them feels their ideas are represented. So if you don't vote, your interests are not represented." Rameen contributed, "So we can give our opinions." Then Judy added, "It's a way of saying what we want," which was followed by Denise's comment, "It's a way to help determine who will be making decisions for the future." Next, Charlotte stated, "It allows us to have a say in who represents us," while Jacob inserted, "It gives us a little control over the government." Mandy then explained, "So that people making the laws will have your best interests in mind." Finally, Kay contributed, "I can voice my opinions, my concerns for the country by how I vote."

When we interviewed the students at the end of the unit about what they learned from the interviews with family members about voting, most understood at least two of the criteria for being eligible to vote today in Wisconsin. They explained that voters must be eighteen years old or older, a U.S. citizen, registered to vote, and not convicted of a felony. They also learned at least one reason why voting is important. The fourth graders offered such reasons as wanting to express how they feel and making their ideas known, doing something important for the community, showing they counted as U.S. citizens, giving their opinion on who should be leaders, and making sure the leaders were good. Rameen explained how his mother emphasized the importance of choosing the leaders through voting:

> She thought voting was important because if you couldn't give your opinion on who should be governor or President, it wouldn't be good for them. You might get a President that you wouldn't want. She said if she couldn't vote, she would feel really bad. Then the person who she didn't want would be the governor or President.[62]

Even though Xee's mother was not a U.S. citizen and eligible to vote, she understood the importance of voting to select leaders who would represent her own interests as a Hmong refugee originally from Laos:

> I interviewed my mom, she wasn't eligible to vote. She wasn't a citizen. She was over twenty-one. [She thought voting was important] because you could choose the person you want that will be smart and make good laws. Not send all the people back to the states or country. [If she couldn't vote], she felt bad because she didn't get to choose who she wanted.[63]

Finally, Denise's mother believed voting was a way to contribute to the broader community:

> It is very important for somebody to be able to vote. It is like your freedom, like you can do something that is important for the whole community. If you couldn't vote, it feels like you are not important. She is doing something important for the community. She is being recognized as a citizen. She helps make decisions for the future.[64]

FOCUS ON YOUR STATE: MAKING VOTING RIGHTS PERSONAL

In order to encourage your students to make personal connections with the significance of voting today, you might:

• Communicate with your students' families about the possibilities of interviewing an adult member of their family about the importance of voting to them. If family members prefer not to be interviewed, arrange for your students to interview members of your school community, such as another teacher, teacher assistant, or secretary.

• Invite a guest speaker from the League of Women Voters to explain the history of this organization as related to women's voting rights, the significance of people's right and responsibility to vote today, and ways the League of Women Voters encourages voting. To gain background information, you might review "Learning from the Suffragists: The League of Women Voters Educates Citizens for Action," and your students might read "The League of Women Voters."[65]

- Invite a guest speaker from a local citizenship class who helps new immigrants prepare for U.S. citizenship. Encourage the guest speaker to explain the importance of citizenship and voting rights to new immigrants in your state.

REFLECTIONS AND RECOMMENDATIONS

The strategy of organizing students into family groups representing different cultures and socioeconomic levels to examine the effects of the transition to statehood on their families was very valuable in promoting students' engagement and learning. Students were actively involved in discussing what they liked and disliked about living in the Northwest Territory, the Wisconsin Territory, and deciding if Wisconsin should become a state. We encourage you to use a similar strategy with your own students to promote thinking about different points of view about becoming a state. You may find, as we did, that elementary students are capable of analyzing from diverse perspectives significant changes as your region moved from a colony or territory toward statehood.

Your students may also evaluate the government's fairness in its treatment of different groups of people during this same period, just as our students examined the rights of Native people, poor immigrant farmers, struggling mining families, land-owning Yankees, and wealthy immigrant landowners. Often elementary students have a strong sense of justice, which is invaluable in analyzing the issue of voting rights. We were impressed with our fourth graders' recommendation that all Wisconsin citizens over eighteen years of age should have the right to vote, have a voice in government, and choose governmental leaders to represent them. A few argued for voting rights for children because they could read and understand the ideas candidates discussed.

As we continue to improve our curriculum unit, we are finding it necessary to devote more time to the statehood voting simulation and follow-up discussion. If you use a voting simulation, we recommend ample discussion about why your students voted as they did and what they learned from the simulation. Our students need opportunities to explain the reasoning for their vote when only the official, qualified voters cast their ballot for statehood and when all adult members of different groups could vote. We believe you, too, will find it valuable to discover why your students choose to follow or ignore what will benefit their family the most in deciding if your colony or territory should become a state. It is gratifying when students can articulate their family's perspective on statehood and also demonstrate a concern for the common good regarding becoming a state.

ENDNOTES

1. *Yankee* was a term used by residents of the Wisconsin territory to denote immigrants from the eastern United States to distinguish them from European immigrants.
2. National Council for the Social Studies, *Expectations of Excellence: Curriculum Standards for Social Studies* (Washington, DC: National Council for the Social Studies, 1994), 63.
3. Hal Balsiger, Paula DeHart, Margaret A. Laughlin, Stephen A. Rose, and Michael Yell, *Planning Curriculum in Social Studies* (Madison, WI: Wisconsin Department of Public Instruction, 2001), 78.
4. National Council for the Social Studies, 73.
5. Balsiger et al., 78.
6. Christine A. Sleeter and Carl A. Grant, *Making Choices for Multicultural Education: Five Approaches to Race, Class, and Gender,* 3rd ed. (Upper Saddle River, NJ: Merrill, 1999), 188–216.
7. Carrie Rothstein-Fisch, Patricia M. Greenfield, and Elise Trumball, "Bridging Cultures with Classroom Strategies," *Educational Leadership* 56 (1999), 64–67.
8. Jere Brophy and Janet Alleman, *Powerful Social Studies for Elementary Students* (New York: Harcourt Brace, 1996), 63–77; Geoffrey Scheurman, "From Behaviorist to Constructivist Teaching," *Social Education* 62 (January, 1998), 6–9.
9. Howard W. Kanetzke, "The Wisconsin Territory," *Badger History* 27 No. 1 (September, 1973): 4–25; Howard W. Kanetzke, "From Northwest Ordinance to Statehood," *Badger History* 29 No. 1 (September, 1975): 52–57; Howard W. Kanetzke, "Wisconsin's Constitution," *Badger History* 32 No. 2 (November, 1978): 4–9; Billie Joan English and

Sharon Cooper Calhoun, *The Wisconsin Story* (Oklahoma City, OK: Apple Corps, 1987), 55–71. Although no longer in print, *Badger History* was a publication designed for fourth graders to use in learning Wisconsin history and published by the State Historical Society of Wisconsin. More recent articles appropriate for fourth graders to learn about the Northwest Territory are: Meg Greene, "The Best System We Could Get," *Cobblestone* 19 No. 7 (October, 1998): 4–7; Ruth Tenzer Feldman, "The Dredful Scott Decision," *Cobblestone* 19 No. 7 (October, 1998): 26–30.

10. Steven Zemelman, Harvey Daniels, and Arthur Hyde, *Best Practice: New Standards for Teaching and Learning in America's Schools* (Portsmouth, NH: Heinemann, 1998), 132–155.
11. Interview with Susan, 1/15/98.
12. Interview with Jim, 1/14/98.
13. Interview with Chia, 1/20/98.
14. Interview with Maria, 1/7/98.
15. Interview with Patty, 1/7/98.
16. Interview with Rameen, 1/7/98.
17. David E. Sahr, "Native American Governments in Today's Curriculum," *Social Education*, 61 No. 6 (October, 1997): 308–315; Karen D. Harvey, Lisa D. Harjo, and Lynda Welborn, *How to Teach About American Indians: A Guide for the School Library Media Specialist* (Westport, CT: Greenwood Press, 1995), 169–180.
18. Meg Greene, "The Best System We Could Get," *Cobblestone*, 19 No. 7 (October, 1998): 4–7.
19. Kanetzke, "The Wisconsin Territory"; Kanetzke, "Wisconsin's Constitution"; English and Calhoun, 74–78; Leslie H. Fishel, "Wisconsin and Negro Suffrage," *Wisconsin Magazine of History*, 46 No. 3 (Spring, 1963): 180–196.
20. Interview with Jacob, 1/14/98.
21. Interview with Jake, 1/13/98.
22. Interview with Neal, 1/21/98.
23. Interview with Patty, 1/7/98.
24. Interview with Mandy, 1/8/98.
25. Interview with Mandy, 1/8/98.
26. Interview with Carlos, 1/8/98.
27. Carolyn Gard, "Elections in the Colonies," *Cobblestone*, 17 No. 7 (October, 1996): 4–9.
28. National Council for the Social Studies, 63.
29. Sleeter and Grant, 188–216.

30. National Council for the Social Studies, 73.
31. Sleeter and Grant, 204–206.
32. Balsiger et al., 78.
33. Carole Edelsky, "Education for Democracy," in JoBeth Allen, ed., *Class Actions: Teaching for Social Justice in Elementary and Middle School* (New York: Teachers College Press, 1999), 147–156; Carole Edelsky, "On Critical Whole Language Practice: Why, What, and a Bit of How," in Carole Edelsky, ed., *Making Justice Our Project: Teachers Working Toward Critical Whole Language Practice* (Urbana, IL: National Council of Teachers of English, 1999), 19–36.
34. Donna C. Creighton, "Critical Literacy in the Elementary Classroom," *Language Arts* 74 (1997), 438–445.
35. Interview with Charlotte, 1/8/98.
36. Interview with Patty, 1/7/98.
37. Interview with Rameen, 1/7/98.
38. Emily Arnold McCully, *The Ballot Box Battle* (New York: Alfred A. Knopf, 1996).
39. Barbara Tomin and Carol Burgoa, *Failure is Impossible: A Susan B. Anthony Biography* (Santa Rosa, CA: Tomin Burgoa Productions, 1983).
40. Interview with Carlos, 1/8/98.
41. Interview with Neal, 1/21/98.
42. Interview with Patty, 1/7/98.
43. Interview with Danny, 1/8/98.
44. Resources for this speech include: Jeri Ferris, *Walking the Road to Freedom: A Story About Sojourner Truth* (Minneapolis, Carolrhoda Books, 1988), 43–45; Peter Krass, *Sojourner Truth: Antislavery Activist* (New York: Chelsea House, 1988), 11–19; Patricia C. McKissack and Frederick McKissack, *Sojourner Truth: Ain't I a Woman?* (New York: Scholastic, 1992), 99–115; Nell Irvin Painter, "Representing Truth: Sojourner Truth's Knowing and Becoming Known," *The Journal of American History*, 81 No. 2 (September, 1994): 488–492. Additional picture books which portray the life of Sojourner Truth include: David A. Adler, *A Picture Book of Sojourner Truth* (New York: Holiday House, 1994) and Anne Rockwell, *Only Passing Through: The Story of Sojourner Truth* (New York: Alfred A. Knopf, 2000).
45. Resources for this summary include: Michael McCurdy, ed., *Escape from Slavery: The Boyhood of Frederick Douglass in His Own Words* (New York: Alfred A. Knopf, 1994); Sharman Russell, "The Early Years," *Cobblestone*, 10 No. 2 (February, 1989): 6–10; Frederick Douglass, "The ABC's," *Cobblestone*, 10 No. 2 (February, 1989): 11–14; Lisa

Belcher-Hamilton, "The Underground Railroad: The Beginning of Douglass's Journey, *Cobblestone*, 10 No. 2 (February, 1989): 15–17; Karen H. Kusek, "Frederick Douglass, Abolitionist Writer," *Cobblestone*, 10 No. 2 (February, 1989): 21–24; Karen E. Hong, "Frederick Douglass and Women's Rights," *Cobblestone*, 10 No. 2 (February, 1989): 25–28. An excellent picture book portraying the early life of Frederick Douglass is William Miller, *Frederick Douglass: The Last Day of Slavery* (New York: Lee & Low Books, 1995).

46. These included the McCurdy text, and several photographs from the February, 1989, issue of *Cobblestone* magazine.

47. Interview with Carlos, 1/8/98.

48. Interview with Denise, 1/13/98.

49. Interview with Carlos, 1/8/98.

50. Victoria Brown, *Uncommon Lives of Common Women: The Missing Half of Wisconsin History* (Madison, WI: Wisconsin Feminists Project Fund, 1975), 29–57; James I. Clark, *Wisconsin Women Fight for Suffrage* (Madison, WI: The State Historical Society of Wisconsin, 1956), 3–19; Fishel, 180–196.

51. The sources of the photographs were the original texts by Brown and Clark on suffrage.

52. Interview with Jake, 1/13/98.

53. Interview with Mandy, 1/8/98.

54. Interview with Neal, 1/21/98.

55. Interview with Tong, 1/20/98.

56. Interview with Charlotte, 1/8/98.

57. George Sullivan, *The Day the Women Got the Vote: A Photo History of the Women's Rights Movement* (New York: Scholastic, 1994); Connie Nordhielm Wooldridge, *When Esther Morris Headed West: Women, Wyoming, and the Right to Vote* (New York: Holiday House, 2001).

58. Kate Connell, *They Shall Be Heard: Susan B. Anthony & Elizabeth Cady Stanton* (Austin, TX: Raintree Steck-Vaughn, 1993); Jeanne Gehret, *Susan B. Anthony: And Justice for All* (Fairport, NY: Verbal Images Press, 1994); Jean Fritz, *You Want Women to Vote, Lizzie Stanton?* (New York: G. P. Putnam's Sons, 1995).

59. McKissack and McKissack; Ferris; Adler; McCurdy.

60. National Council for the Social Studies, 73.

61. Sleeter and Grant, 188–216; Zemelman et al., 132–155.

62. Interview with Rameen, 1/7/98.

63. Interview with Xee, 1/15/98.

64. Interview with Denise, 1/13/98.

65. Becky Cain, "Learning from the Suffragists: The League of Women Voters Educates Citizens for Action," *Social Education*, 59 No. 5 (September, 1995): 290–292; Lisa Belcher-Hamilton, "The League of Women Voters," *Cobblestone*, 9 No. 11 (November, 1988): 35–36.

CHAPTER 5

LEARNING ABOUT STATE INDUSTRIES

Charlotte and Danny placed copies of old photographs on the board illustrating lumbering activities during the nineteenth and early twentieth century.[1] They elaborated on the meanings of the photographs for the rest of the class. Each small group of fourth graders received several photographs or drawings of daily activities in a lumber camp, the removal of lumber from the woods, the transportation of logs down the river, or the movement of logs into sawmills. We asked the students to put the photographs or drawings in an order that made sense to them and then tell a story about them. With some additional guidance from the two of us and Kristen, our research assistant, each group discussed what was happening in the photographs or drawings, decided on the sequence of activities, and rehearsed their class presentation.

Danny and Charlotte expanded on their sequence of photographs to show daily life in a lumber camp during their presentation.

Charlotte: This is a picture of a lumbering crew with their tools after the trees are marked and they're ready to cut them down.

Danny: There's a lunch sleigh they use to bring food to the workers every day at noon.

Charlotte: This is a picture of a wood butcher or carpenter and a blacksmith working.

Danny: This is a picture of a cookee or cooks and they're getting the tables ready for dinner for the men.

Charlotte: They had fun at night. They would have a fiddler and a jigger and they would have fun doing that before they went to bed.

Danny: This one is the [reads the caption] "lumberjacks in bunk-house." That's where they sleep and everything.

Charlotte: They get up in the morning and they go out and wash their clothes and then they hang them outside to dry. They had kind of a boring life. All you have to do is work all day and then at night you only get a little bit of time to have fun.

Susan, Jake, and Rameen also presented their interpretation of drawings illustrating life in a lumber camp.[2] They chose to add drama to their explanation of the drawings.

Susan: Blacksmiths shoe horses and oxen and repair metal tools. (Rameen and Jake dramatized hammering.)

Rameen: Scrubbing and boiling clothes clean and hanging them out to freeze dry is a regular Sunday chore. (Susan and Jake pantomimed scrubbing clothes, wringing them out, and hanging them up to dry.)

Jake: A lumberjack buys a new shirt from the camp foreman. The boss keeps track in company books of the number of logs cut that day. (Susan dramatized purchasing a shirt and trying it on while Rameen gleefully counted the money received for the purchase.)

Jake: The lumberjacks are eating here. It looks like they're not talking, looks like they got pie there and other stuff. It looks like they're hungry. (Susan and Rameen pantomimed eating very quickly.)

Susan: In this picture it looks like they're having fun by dancing and singing. The men are wearing aprons pretending to be women so that they can partner dance. (Jake and Rameen dramatized dancing by linking arms and dancing in a circle, then changing arms and dancing in the opposite direction. Jake held out his shirt and curtsied while members of the class giggled.)

Rameen: At the end lumberjacks are all sleeping. All the wet clothes they were wearing they hung up to dry. (Jake and Susan placed their heads on their hands to dramatize sleeping.)

Following each small group presentation, the rest of the class asked questions to clarify their understanding of ideas offered in the presentation. The analysis and presentation of photographs or drawings was one important strategy to help the fourth graders learn more about lumbering during the nineteenth and early twentieth centuries, one of the early industries in our state. For our final state history unit, we not only wanted students to learn about the lumber and paper industries and wheat and dairy farming, but we wanted them to examine the industries from the perspective of workers. We hoped the fourth graders would appreciate worker contributions, including the physically demanding tasks and dangerous conditions under which many workers labored. In contrast to the romanticization of the life of a lumberjack through Paul Bunyan tall tales, we encouraged the students to understand and empathize with the risky, difficult realities involved with lumbering.

STUDYING THE LUMBER INDUSTRY FROM WORKER PERSPECTIVES

Addressing Standards, Multicultural Ideas, and Best Teaching Practices

Although we hoped students would learn about the lumber industry and its importance in state history, we focused on workers' perspectives and experiences rather than those of lumber barons or lumber industry owners. We provided opportunities for students to learn about lumber camp activities, the removal of trees from the forests, the movement of logs down the river to a saw mill, and the processing of the lumber at the sawmills—all from the perspectives of the workers. This emphasis was congruent with the current trend in social studies education to concentrate on social history or the activities of ordinary people.[3] Our attention to lumber industry workers was also compatible with the multicultural education emphasis on addressing classism within the curriculum and include the experiences and perspectives of people with low socioeconomic status, such as lumber workers.[4] Typically, when social studies texts addressed industry, they focused on the experiences of powerful, wealthy industrialists who created industries rather than the contributions, difficulties, and dangers of workers who kept industries functioning.

Our focus on lumber industry workers' experiences and per-spectives also addressed national, state, and local social studies stan-dards and school district literacy objectives. We concentrated on the national social studies thematic strand People, Places, and Environ-ments.[5] Our goal was for students to learn how the state's physical environment of forests and rivers provided the natural resources for the development of the lumber industry. As the lumber industry grew and resulted in clear-cutting heavily forested areas and polluting rivers with lumber debris, the state's physical environment changed signif-icantly. This national thematic strand corresponded to the state and local Geography: People, Places, and Environments standard:

• Students will describe and give examples of ways in which people in-teract with the physical environment, including use of land, location of communities, methods of construction, and design of shelters.[6]

For the Production, Distribution, and Consumption thematic strand,[7] we provided opportunities for students to learn that lumber was the most important industry in Wisconsin during 1890–1920 and that lumber was harvested for consumption within the state and throughout the United States. We also concentrated on the impor-tance and skills of workers to these industries in order to produce needed lumber while the industries offered a source of income for workers to meet their basic needs. Through these opportunities, we also addressed specific state and local standards regarding Economics: Production, Exchange, and Consumption.

• Students will identify local goods that are part of the global econ-omy and explain their use in Wisconsin.

• Students will give examples how businesses and industry depend on workers with specialized skills to make production more efficient.[8]

Finally, we incorporated the Time, Continuity, and Change[9] national social studies thematic strand by providing different strate-gies and resources for students to learn about life in the past, espe-cially lumber industry workers' lives during the nineteenth and early twentieth centuries in the state. Through a history workshop approach[10] which integrated analysis of old lumbering photographs and drawings, a presentation by a local historian on the lumber industry, and reading about life as a lumberjack through a picture book, we provided opportunities for the fourth graders to meet local and state standards regarding History: Time, Continuity, and Change:

• Students will examine various sources of information that are used for constructing the past.

• Students will examine biographies, stories, narratives, and folktales to understand the lives of ordinary and extraordinary people, place them in time and context, and explain their relationship to important historical events.[11]

School district literacy objectives and best teaching practices were also incorporated in our unit on lumbering. We read, discussed, and responded in writing to the well-illustrated trade book *Lumberjack*[12] and students worked in small groups to analyze and present their interpretation of drawings and photographs of the lumber industry.

LEARNING THROUGH PHOTOGRAPHS, COMMUNITY RESOURCES, AND TRADE BOOKS: A HISTORY WORKSHOP APPROACH

We used a history workshop approach to provide several important opportunities for the fourth graders to work together constructing knowledge about the lumber industry. A history workshop involves the use of primary sources, such as photographs, along with history stories to develop an understanding of times past.[13] For our history workshop, we used authentic photographs of lumbering in Wisconsin and historically accurate drawings of lumbering in Wisconsin and Minnesota during the nineteenth and early twentieth centuries as our primary sources.[14] We listened to stories told by a local historian about the lumber industry in the state and in our own city of Oshkosh based on his research and his father's experiences as a worker in a lumber mill during the early twentieth century. We read about one man's experiences working in a lumber camp in Canada in 1940–1950 in the well-illustrated trade book *Lumberjack*.[15] Students learned about different aspects of lumber workers' experiences in lumber camps and the dangers involved in cutting trees and removing them from the woods, driving lumber down rivers, and cutting lumber into boards in sawmills.

Analysis of Photographs and Drawings

All students worked in small groups to study, sequence, and interpret several photographs or drawings about the lumber industry for the rest of the class, shown in Figure 5–1. In addition to the opening description of the fourth graders' presentations of life in a lumber camp, another small group, Judy and Maria, presented their photographs[16] illustrating the process of cutting trees and removing them from the forest. Their presentation and the class discussion exemplified how we and the fourth graders cooperatively constructed an understanding of how lumber workers hauled logs from the woods.

Judy: They're cutting the tree. [They] girdle the tree, take off a line of bark.

Maria: On this one, they yell "Timber!" to tell people that the tree is falling.

Judy: And then they cut the tree between.

Maria: They're putting some wood on the sled.

Judy: On this one, they have a load of logs, which is pretty old fashioned because they have a sled and horses are taking it.

Ava: Remember this was over 100 years ago, so they were still using horses then.

Maria: In this picture they're pulling the sled. [When] the road goes down, they put straw under the sled to keep it from going too fast.

Ava: That was a problem. If the road was sort of going downhill a little bit, it could go faster and faster and faster and get out of control.

FIGURE 5–1 Students share their interpretations of lumber industry photographs

People could be hurt. The wood could just fall off and it could be really dangerous. The horses could be hurt.

Jacob: Or killed.

Ava: Or killed.

Judy: Another picture, they had a water tank. They throw water on the road so if it's really cold, it turns to ice and makes hauling wood easier.

Maria: In this picture, put the logs in the water for the winter, then when the ice melts in the spring, the logs would float down. When the ice melts the logs go to the sawmill.

Thelma: They float down the river, right.

John: [Questioning an earlier photograph] They put water on it because they're going downhill?

Ava: I think they generally watered it [the logging road] a little bit to keep it slippery and to make it easier to travel. I think they would water it less on hills. You're right because that wouldn't make any sense to have it real icy when it could be so slippery going downhill.

Thelma: I think they just did that on flat land, particularly when the snow would be soft. What would happen? Think about the times you go sledding and you're going on soft snow. You could pull the sled and when you sit on the sled, then what happens?

Charlotte: It goes down.

Thelma: It goes down and it's harder to pull. They did that more on the flat areas. They wouldn't have to do it quite as much when it was going down, right?

Carlos: Why do you think the men are standing on the logs [referring to a photograph of men standing on a tall load of logs placed on a sled pulled by horses]?

Judy: They're probably proud that they got all that done. And they get to go back and get the rest of the logs. And then they're done for the day.

Ava: Some think they're trying to show off for the camera because they couldn't normally travel that way. If they were going to take the lumber out of the woods, there would not be men standing on top because that would be too dangerous. I think they ended up doing that for the camera.

Rameen: What was that little black shady part in the second picture?

Judy: I'm not really sure.

Thelma: Isn't that the top of the tree toppling over? That's some of the branches sticking out like a Christmas tree.

Ava: It's [the photograph] sort of blurry because the tree's falling down.

Stories from a Community Historian

We invited Clarence Jungwirth, a local historian, to speak to the class about workers' experiences in lumber camps and lumber mills. Clarence had written several books about Oshkosh history, completed extensive research on the lumber industry in Wisconsin and the significance of lumbering to the growth of Oshkosh in the nineteenth century, and had personal knowledge of lumber mills through his father's experiences as a lumber mill worker. Clarence was also an excellent history resource for children. He made history come alive through stories. The fourth graders listened attentively to Clarence's presentation and asked many questions afterwards. Clarence described what it was like to work in lumber camps and lumber mills.

Community Historian's Lumber Camp Story

When immigrants came to Wisconsin, they worked in the lumber industry. They cut trees down beginning in the 1850s and 1860s. The only time they could work in the lumber camps was in the winter because the people who worked in lumber mills went up in September and stayed until April or until the snow melted. They cut trees in winter. Do you know how they cut trees? [Denise replied, "They used axes," and Jacob added, "Saws."] The length of saws would be from the front of the room to near the back of the room with one man on each end. Can you imagine sawing through a tree this big [pointed to two desks pushed together]? Sometimes it would take them all day to saw a tree down because it was so big. They might have a 250-foot tree, chop or saw it down, and then they'd have to chop or saw the log into pieces 18–20 feet long to handle it. If two men cut a tree in one day, they were doing a good job.

For those who worked in logging camps, they made $21 a month. There would be big log cabins, 50–60 feet long, with bunks in them. The people who worked in lumber camps would have to get up at the crack of dawn, work until they couldn't see anymore, and come back. In the winter time in northern Wisconsin, they might have three to five feet of snow on the ground. They had to go way back in the woods and track through all the snow. It was cold, sometimes 30–40 degrees below zero. They'd still have to work. They had a rough time. A lot of people who worked in the lumber camps got sick often. They only had one day off on Sundays. That's when they mended clothes, washed clothes, took a bath. If they were lucky they could take a bath. Sometimes people that worked in lumber camps like this wouldn't take a bath for six months. Water was scarce in lumber camps and the way they got water was to melt snow. It took a long time to melt snow. You'd have sixty men in a room; think of the amount of snow you'd have to melt to wash clothes and take a bath. Some men who didn't care about washing clothes kept them on for about six months. They would take them off to go to bed at night and sleep.

Community Historian's Lumber Mill Story

The only work available in Oshkosh in the 1860s and 1870s was work in lumber mills. The pay in 1870 from working 6 A.M. to 6 P.M., twelve hours a day, was ninety-six cents a day. In Oshkosh in those days, people were poor. My father worked in a lumber mill for fifty years and lived on the south side of Oshkosh. Do you know where the Paine Museum is? [Several students replied, "Yes."] That was the biggest lumber mill in Oshkosh and employed over two thousand people at that time. My dad lived one-and-a-half miles away from the mill. Even though they had street cars in Oshkosh, my dad was so poor, he couldn't afford the street car, so he had to walk to work. He had to get up about four in the morning, have breakfast, and walk an hour to work. That was six days a week. The workers only got time off for lunch, one hour.

There was no electricity in Oshkosh in the 1860s. The motors [in the lumber mills] were run by gasoline. Each motor was connected to sawing machines. It was noisy with all the saws running at the same time. They didn't have ear plugs in those days. A lot of people who worked in the lumber mills for a long period of time became deaf. The noise was constant.

It was mostly men who worked in the mills in the 1860s and 1870s. My dad had to go to work when he was twelve years old. To go to school was considered a waste of time back in the early part of lumbering. If you were a boy working in a lumber mill, you got paid sixty-five cents a day for a twelve hour day. Women weren't hired because women weren't supposed to work. Women were supposed to stay home. It was mostly young men and boys who worked in lumber mills.

For a lot of people, it was very dangerous work with saws. A lot of people had their arms cut off, fingers cut off, hands cut off. If you got your hand cut off, there was no hospitalization. You had to pay for it yourself to take care of it. Like my dad one time got his whole arm chewed up in the saw. He couldn't work and he had to pay for it all himself. There were a lot of accidents. If you lost a hand or arm, that meant you were poor for the rest of your life because you couldn't work. Nobody [your employer or the government] took care of you. In those days, if you didn't work, you didn't eat, but people helped each other out more in those days. If you couldn't work, you depended on your relatives. There were an awful lot of accidents in the mills.

Reading a Lumberjack's Story

In addition to the stories told by a community historian, we read a lumber worker's story in the picture book *Lumberjack* during our history workshop. The text portrayed the author's memories of his experiences of working in a lumber camp and driving logs down rivers in Canada in the 1940s and 1950s. When we introduced the book to the class, we clarified that the author was a lumberjack at a later time than our focus on lumbering in Wisconsin during the nineteenth and early twentieth centuries and that his lumbering experiences occurred in Canada, north of our state. However, many of Kurelek's experiences were similar to Wisconsin immigrant lumber camp workers. The author is also a painter and included many beautiful paintings depicting numerous aspects of life in lumber camps in the text. The illustrations were especially helpful for struggling readers to construct an understanding of main ideas from the text. We offered different avenues for students to read the text, including individually, with an audiotaped recording of the text (shown in Figure 5–2), with a partner, or with one of us. We led class discussions about main ideas in the book, then asked students to respond to the text in their journals. As students read and discussed the text with us, we encouraged them to read to learn more about the dangerous aspects of a lumberjack's job, the difficulties of cutting trees in the rain or snow, how the author might have felt about being a lumberjack, and the author's purpose in writing the text. The fourth graders were also encouraged to speculate about what their lives would be like as lumber camp workers and what they would like and dislike about the experience.

In our closing class discussion on the lumber industry's effects on our state, we asked students to summarize how this early industry helped and hurt people. Students were encouraged to understand that the industry provided needed income for workers and wood for building homes, but the dangerous conditions in lumber camps and

FIGURE 5–2 Some students choose to read with an audiotaped version of *Lumberjack*

mills resulted in many worker injuries and deaths. As we discussed the effects on the environment, we emphasized that at that time, the lumber industry clear-cut forested areas without replanting trees, resulting in the destruction of old-growth forests in the northern part of our state. Rivers became polluted with debris when logs were moved down river and when sawdust and bark were dumped into rivers. However, the lumber industry also helped the state's economy and led to the growth of several cities, including Oshkosh. Beginning in the 1920s, foresters began to rebuild northern Wisconsin forests.

"It Was a Hard Life": Work in Lumber Camps

During interviews with students at the end of the unit, we were pleased to discover that the fourth graders learned about many of the challenges for workers in lumber camps. They recognized and empathized with the long days, hard work, tedious daily and weekly work schedule, and limited recreation. Carlos described some of the challenges for lumber camp workers:

> It was a hard life. You would have to be out there for awhile if you wanted to get paid good. You would have to sleep in the same room as other people. You would have bugs in your bed and that wouldn't be so good. They got fed good. Cooks and cookees would work in the kitchen. The cookees would do whatever the cooks said. I think they got paid more than the lumberjacks. Men and boys usually worked in lumber camps. Some women would work as a cook. In the morning they would get fed good. They would get fed good all through the day. If they missed breakfast, they weren't going to keep it hot for you. You would have to get up in the morning and if you didn't feel like eating, you would have to starve until lunch time. You couldn't talk in the dining room. They just wanted you to go in there and eat so you can get your strength ready to go and cut down trees.[17]

Jake understood lumber workers' daily and weekly routines, which included a great deal of work, few comforts, and little time for fun:

> They would have to get up at dawn or sunrise, get ready, go to the breakfast house, eat as much as they could, go out and work until sundown, come back, eat, and go to bed, and do the same thing every morning. There was a bathing time on Sunday. They only took a bath once a week. When their stuff got wet, they would hang it on little wires by a fireplace [stove] or by their beds so they would dry. Their bunk beds weren't very comfortable because of the straw. There was no cushion. Men usually worked in lumber camps. In the 1800s they started to let women in to cook. In the 1800s they would have men work because they thought women should stay home and raise kids and do women things. Men should do men things. They could only have fun one night out of the whole week. They did the basics. Go to bed, wake up, work all day, come home, eat, go to bed.[18]

"Timber!" Challenges of Cutting Trees and Hauling Logs Out of the Woods

When students were questioned about what they learned about lumbering during individual interviews at the end of the unit, a few described some of the processes of cutting down trees and removing them from the forests. Xee recounted some of the steps lumber workers followed in cutting down a tree:

> They would have to cut a little slit through the tree. One man would take the saw and rub it back and forth until it was ready to fall. They could call "Timber!" The other men would have to call it really loud, so if it [the tree] was really big, the other men wouldn't get hurt. They measure the tree and they cut off the leaves. They have a kind of strap [to use to determine] how they were going to cut it. They mark the company's name on it [the tree].[19]

Although most students did not voice their concern about the clear-cutting that resulted from the lumber industry's presence in northern Wisconsin, Jim explained the problem with cutting too many trees as well as how trees were moved out of the forest:

> They shouldn't have cut down as much as they did. They cut down too much. They didn't leave any forest like in this picture here [pointing to a picture on the bulletin board of a clear-cut area of northern Wisconsin]. It might not grow back for the future. It might still be bare and people might not like it. The trails could be hard for the horses to pull the sled [of logs] on. They would have one [sled] with a water filling tank. It would dribble water on the road so it would make it icy.[20]

"It Was a Dangerous Job": Moving Logs Down River

From the history workshop, several fourth graders learned about the dangers of moving logs by river from the forested areas of the state to a lumber mill. During individual interviews at the close of the unit, students described how logs were transported. Patty provided a concise summary:

> You [lumber camps] would have to be close to a river so you can send down the logs to the lumber mills. They would chop down a tree and send it with a horse and an oxen. First they had oxen, then they found horses moved faster. They used horses. They took them down to the river's edge. Men would take them out and put them in the river. They would float down. Sometimes there was a jam and they would have to blow it up with dynamite or try to move it themselves.

The dynamite would hurt the logs. Then they ended up with them in the lumber mill. There they would have to sort them out to see which logs belong to which companies.[21]

Charlotte described some of the dangers for lumber workers who moved the logs down river:

It was a hard job trying to get all the wood in the river. It was all piled up so high because they cut so much during the winter time to send down the river to the factory. It was a dangerous job to be in the water when they had the wood in there. It could sink the guys in the water if all the wood was coming really fast at them. There were a lot of jams because there was a lot of wood, especially when you first put it in the water. They had so much falling into the water at one time. They probably had a lot of people there so it wouldn't jam up. The men had long poles. They would have to stand on the river and push the lumber so it would keep going in a straight line and wouldn't get in a jam. When they had a jam, they had to blow it up. There always had to be a few people in boats to be closer to the wood in case of a jam. They could get there quicker. They had to separate the wood when it got to the factories.[22]

"It Wasn't a Safe Place": Work in Lumber Mills

During interviews at the end of the unit, most of the fourth graders understood that working in a lumber mill was a very dangerous job. Charlotte knew why men and boys worked in lumber mills despite the dangers:

A lot of people worked there [lumber mills] because it was one of the main ways to make money back then. A lot of people went deaf and had fingers cut off or hurt badly because of the machines.[23]

Xee especially was concerned about boys working in dangerous lumber mills and the consequences from injuries:

Working in a lumber camp is better than working in a lumber mill. The twelve-year-old boys had to go and work in the lumber mill. It was really dangerous for kids until twelve. It would be really bad for them to cut off their hand or their skin. Mr. Jungwirth said his dad had mostly all of his skin cut off on his arm. The saw almost cut off his whole arm. His dad had to stay home for a week or a month. It needed time to heal. They couldn't work anymore. They were poor.[24]

FOCUS ON YOUR STATE:
EARLY INDUSTRIES

In preparation for teaching about early industries in your state, you might contact state and local historical societies for identification of the most important first industries and why they were so significant to your state's history. To locate additional teaching resources, you might:

• Contact museums, historical sites, and state and local historical societies for suggestions of guest speakers, field trips, artifacts, photographs, videos, websites, children's texts and other print documents which portray early industries. Request resources depicting workers' experiences and perspectives in early industries to compare and contrast with those of industry owners.

• Review recommendations of trade books for children and youth for examples of texts which deal with your state's first industries. For example, the annotated list of Notable Social Studies Trade Books for Young People is published annually in the April/May or June/July issue of *Social Education* and many valuable texts are described in *Children's Literature in Social Studies: Teaching to the Standards* and *Linking Literature with Life: The NCSS Standards and Children's Literature for the Middle Grades.*[25]

• Contact environmental organizations in your state, such as the department of natural resources or your state's branch of the National Wildlife Federation for suggestions of guest speakers, field trips, photographs, children's texts, and other print documents which illustrate the impact of early industries on your state's physical environment.

In order to encourage critical literacy among your students, you might include a comparison and contrast of two different trade books, one illustrating an early state industry and another dealing with the industry's environmental impact or harmful effect on workers. For example, if your state included lumbering as an early industry, you might have your students read both *The Lumberjack* and *The Lorax*,[26] compare the author's purpose in each text, the values and activities of the main characters, and which groups benefited and which suffered from the main events in the text. Your students might analyze how people in your state can balance the need for economic activities to enable people to earn a living and produce needed services and goods with care for the environment and the provision of safe, humane working environments.

PAPER INDUSTRY'S ENVIRONMENTAL CONCERNS: STANDARDS AND COMMUNITY RESOURCES

When we shifted our attention from lumber to the paper industry, we moved from the past to the present. However, we maintained our focus on the connection between industry and Wisconsin's physical environment. We wanted the fourth graders to understand that the paper industry depended on the state's natural resources in order to flourish. Many paper and pulp mills were located on rivers, especially the nearby Fox River, to take advantage of the water power and water needed during paper and pulp production. We also concentrated on the paper industry's harmful effects on the environment during the twentieth century as well as current efforts by the paper industry to use environmentally safe practices. Finally, we hoped students would learn about the significance of the paper industry to our state in producing more paper products than any other state within the United States, providing needed paper products for individuals and businesscs, and in supplying well-paying jobs for a significant number of workers.

As we studied the state's paper industry, we addressed the same People, Places, and Environments national social studies thematic strand and the corresponding state and local school district performance standards as we did during our investigation of the lumber industry.[27] Students were introduced to a map showing the location of paper and pulp mills along the Fox River from Oshkosh to Green Bay to emphasize the importance of rivers as a natural resource for producing pulp or paper. Simultaneously with learning how paper was produced, the fourth graders understood the significance of water in the paper-making process.

We also addressed the same Production, Distribution, and Consumption national thematic strand and state and local school district standards for the paper industry as we did for the lumber industry.[28] Students had opportunities to discover that Wisconsin produced paper products not only for consumers within the state, but throughout the country. Students learned that workers within the paper industry were paid well for their contributions.

Paper Industry Community Resource

We were fortunate to discover an excellent guest speaker for one of the paper companies within the Fox Valley, where most paper industries were located. Jeff Johnson, the guest speaker, also served as the public relations director for his company, Wisconsin Tissue.[29] During his presentation, Jeff showed some of the paper products his company produced, explained the process of making paper from recycled paper, and described some of the company's environmentally conscious practices. Jeff's visual aids, samples, and clear explanations provided a good learning opportunity for the fourth graders. The students enjoyed handling and inspecting the many visual aids and paper products Jeff introduced, as shown in Figure 5–3. After showing some of the paper products Wisconsin Tissue made, including bathroom tissue, paper towels, and napkins, Jeff described how his company made paper from recovered paper.

Community Resource: Making Paper from Recycled Materials

A lot of paper is made from virgin fiber, from a tree, but Wisconsin Tissue doesn't do that. We recycle the fiber. When you make paper from trees, what you do is actually cut down the tree, take the bark off, take the wood and make it into smaller chips. Then they grind it so it's smaller chips, put it in a big kettle, add chemicals and water, and heat it. They actually cook it so you get your paper fiber from that.

180

FIGURE 5–3 Students examine paper products made from recycled materials following Mr. Johnson's presentation

Part of the process of the way Wisconsin Tissue does it is similar. We use recovered paper. These are a couple of bags with samples of different types of grades of waste paper we use [held up clear plastic bags filled with waste paper]. If you have some paper you're going to throw out, you'll put it in an area to recycle. Well, some of that paper may end up at Wisconsin Tissue's plant. We'll take all kinds of different grades of paper and recycle that. Some of that paper has already been used, like the paper you throw out, like a letter your mom or dad read at home and then put into recycling. We'll take that paper and recycle it in our operation. We buy waste paper through a whole network of dealers and brokers all over the country who generally take paper and sort it into different grades and bale it in the big bales. We take that and use it in our operation.

We'll put it into a big vessel or kettle called a pulper. We do the same thing they do with virgin fiber. We add water, steam, and some chemicals. The idea is to take waste paper and break it up so we can make usable fiber from it. What comes out of the pulper is pulp, what we use to send to the paper machine to make into paper. I often liken it to oatmeal [showed a small glass jar partially filled with gray, semiliquid matter]. Did anybody have oatmeal for breakfast? This looks a little bit like oatmeal to me, although I wouldn't be inclined to eat it. This is the fiber that comes out of that pulper. What we do is add a lot of water to it and then we pump this material onto a moving screen, like the screen door you probably have at your home over your doors or windows. Most of the water drops through that screen and that's where a sheet of paper is actually formed [held up a sheet of "rough" paper]. It's hard for you to picture this, but the whole paper machine is sometimes as long as a football field [showed a picture of paper coming off a paper machine]. I assume most of you are Packer fans, so you could identify with the length of the football field. These machines are really big.

Community Resource: Protecting the Environment

Besides making recycled products, Wisconsin Tissue does a lot of other things to protect the environment. Not only do we have recycled waste paper, but we also recycle our cases, oil we might use, light bulbs that have burned out and have materials in them that can be recycled, ink buckets that are used for ink to print napkins, metal, plastic, and poly materials. We work real hard to reduce waste. Not only does that protect the environment, but it also saves money. So it makes good sense for any business to reduce waste. We work real hard to clean the water we use in our operation. We take water from Little Lake Buttes des Morts in Menasha and clean it. We often brag that the water we send back to the lake is actually cleaner than the water we take out of the lake. We have a program for employees to bring waste paper from home, like newspapers that they have read at home, and bring it into our operation. We recycle it so it doesn't end up in the landfill.

A Story: "Wisconsin's Paper Industry Is the Best!"

In order to provide additional learning opportunities for students and integrate literacy with social studies, we searched for trade books dealing with the paper industry. Unfortunately, we could find no published materials suitable for fourth graders describing the paper industry, its effect on the environment, and workers' experiences.[30] However, two of Ava's former social studies methods students created an interesting story about the paper industry in a short booklet, "Wisconsin's Paper Industry Is the Best!" based on their research on the local paper industry. The students used the booklet in a social studies unit on the paper industry they taught in a fourth-grade classroom and found children learned from it. After gaining permission to use it, we distributed the booklet to small groups of students to read and discuss. Many ideas reinforced Jeff Johnson's presentation. The narrative described the number of paper mills in Wisconsin, how much paper was produced, different jobs in the industry, and the commitment the local paper industry made to taking care of the environment. It explained that participating companies promised to replant trees, prevent pollution, and recycle.

"They Make Lots of Different Types of Paper": Paper Industry Products

During interviews with the fourth graders at the close of the unit, we discovered that several students learned about some of the different paper products made by the local paper industry. Some also described some of the steps in the paper-making process. Denise clarified her impression of the paper industry and its significance following our study:

> It [paper industry] has improved a lot and they make lots of different types of paper. You usually think of a paper mill as old-fashioned and small. It actually was quite big to hold those machines. It is actually quite advanced with all the robots. I didn't think cardboard is a type of paper, but he [Mr. Johnson] taught me it is a type of paper. This was a big corporation. You think that you use paper everyday, bathroom tissue and napkins and facial tissue. It is big. I thought that was neat.[31]

Jim described some of the steps in the paper-making process, the importance of workers' contributions in producing paper, and some of the paper products made:

> Paper mills have many workers to get the job done. They have machines that are as long as two football fields. We learned how they

make the paper. They have these screen things and they pour the mixture over it. They heat it and then it dries out on it. They pull it off and roll it on a roll. They use computers to make designs on napkins and paper towels. The paper they make is called "Second Nature Plus." They used recycled paper so they called it "Second Nature Plus." I think nature means recycled and second also means recycled.[32]

"Helping Nature Stay Clean": Paper Industry's Environmental Protection Practices

Several fourth graders were impressed with the environmentally conscious practices the local paper industry currently implemented. During the unit, we viewed a video on the history of the paper industry and discussed some of the environmental problems resulting from paper production, including water and air pollution and a shortage of timber. Both the guest speaker and the original booklet emphasized how the paper industry today is attempting to compensate for the industry's harmful effects on the environment during earlier times. Carlos summarized some of these environmentally conscious practices:

> Wisconsin Tissue is very concerned about nature. The water [returned to the lake] was cleaner than when it came in[to the factory]. They were paying a lot of money to help nature stay clean. Since the building is by other houses, they send someone over to see if it is too loud or noisy. They use recycled paper or magazines that were cut up. They use it for paper.[33]

Susan was especially pleased to discover that paper companies were replanting trees as part of their efforts to care for the environment:

> They had a project called "Second Nature Plus" because it came out of nature and the product was used again. They are trying to put more trees back into the ground because they are taking them out. And we probably won't have any trees left in a generation maybe even to breathe. That is why they are putting some of them back into the ground.[34]

"We're Number One in Paper": The Significance of the Paper Industry

The end-of-the-unit interviews with the fourth graders also illustrated that several understood the significance of the paper industry for our state. It provided paper products which people and businesses needed, furnished more paper products than any other state in the United States, and supplied jobs for workers. Patty explained what was important about the paper industry for Wisconsin:

> Wisconsin produces the most paper than any other state in the United States. They produce more than five million [tons of paper each year]. They just make the most paper. There is a lot of states that have a lot of paper, but Wisconsin produces the most. It [paper industry] employed a lot of people. You have the paper makers in the paper factories to make the paper. You have the forest workers to cut down the trees. So you employ a lot of people when you do this. Wisconsin is the number one state that produces paper because we produce the most. We also recycle, so that is good.[35]

Carlos summarized his interpretation of the reasons for the significance of paper to our state in producing needed paper products while caring for the environment:

> They make different products. Wisconsin produces most of the paper used in the United States. There are fifty paper mills in Wisconsin. They make the most paper. Every time they cut down a tree they put two in. They pay thousands of dollars to help the forests and the earth. Recycling is very helpful. Recycling helps nature. They help the environment a lot and they just don't care about the business. They care about nature, too. After flour [mills], making paper was a big part of Wisconsin history. A lot of people worked in the mills. It is important because a lot of people need paper to use.[36]

FOCUS ON YOUR STATE: CURRENT INDUSTRIES

In order to identify the most important businesses and industries in your state today, contact your state department of commerce or state chamber of commerce or visit their websites. For significant local businesses and industries, contact or view the websites of your local chamber of commerce or city or county government. Once you know the names of the main businesses or industries in your state or community, you might select one to focus on.

• Contact the public relations department of the industry itself for teaching resources, such as guest speakers, videos, photographs, websites, curriculum guides, texts, and other print documents. Clarify the criteria for appropriate guest speakers for your students: explains the industry in appropriate language for elementary students; uses visual aids to supplement verbal explanations; invites student participation in the presentation; and responds respectfully to students' questions.

• Survey your students' families for family members who have been employed in the industry and invite them to speak to the class about their experiences as workers. Ask the family guest speaker to describe what the industry produces, the industry's importance to the state, the specific job the guest speaker holds, and the benefits and drawbacks of working in the industry. If no family members can serve as guest speakers giving worker perspectives on the industry, contact the industry's labor union for suggestions of guest speakers and other teaching resources.

• Contact local and state environmental groups, such as the department of natural resources and your state's branch of the National Wildlife Federation for background information on the industry's impact on the environment. Ask for teaching resources which describe the physical resources the industry uses and examples of the industry's beneficial or harmful effects on the physical environment of your state.

• Encourage critical literacy among your students with reading about current industry's positive as well as detrimental effects on your state. Look for appropriate trade books about your state's main industry by seeking suggestions from the industry itself, the annotated list of Notable Social Studies Trade Books for Young People published annually in *Social Education* and the recommended texts described in

Children's Literature in Social Studies: Teaching to the Standards and *Linking Literature with Life: The NCSS Standards and Children's Literature for the Middle Grades.*[37] For states with current industries built along rivers (such as the paper industry), your students might read *A River Ran Wild*[38] which portrays the pollution of a river through dumping pulp, dyes, and fibers and actions of citizens to stop the pollution and clean the river.

FROM WHEAT TO DAIRY FARMING

For the closing portion of our unit on state industries, we wanted students to learn about the growth and decline of wheat farming during the nineteenth century, the increase in dairy farming during the late nineteenth and early twentieth centuries, and current challenges in dairy farming. Our focus on farming allowed us to address several national, state, and local social studies standards while using culturally relevant, best teaching practices to engage all students in constructing knowledge.

Our concentration on how farming changed from the nineteenth century to contemporary times allowed us to incorporate the Time, Continuity, and Change[39] national social studies thematic strand. We provided opportunities for students to learn about the different tasks and tools associated with wheat farming during the nineteenth century, how wheat farming changed because of better tools and machines, and the ethos of cooperation among wheat farmers in plowing, harvesting, and threshing. The fourth graders also had opportunities to understand that the growth of dairy farming was due significantly to the invention of the silo in the late nineteenth century. Silos stored silage or food for dairy cattle through the winter months to keep them producing milk. Prior to the construction of silos, farmers had no way to reserve food for cows to eat during the winter, which meant cows did not generate milk. When refrigerated railroad cars also became available during the late nineteenth century, Wisconsin farmers began shipping their dairy products around the country. These goals corresponded to several state and local social studies standards regarding History: Time, Continuity, and Change. We provided opportunities for students to:

• Compare and contrast contemporary life with life in the past, looking at social, economic, political, and cultural roles played by individuals and groups.

• Compare past and present technologies related to energy, transportation, and communications and describe the effects of technological change, either beneficial or harmful, on people and the environment.

• Describe examples of cooperation and interdependence among individuals, groups, and nations.[40]

We also addressed the People, Places, and Environments[41] national social studies thematic strand by introducing students to how the state's physical environment provided the necessary soil and climate for growing wheat and other crops needed to feed dairy cattle. In addition, the state's soil, climate, and terrain allowed for cultivation of pastures for grazing dairy cattle. Another goal was for students to understand that changes in the physical environment led to the decline of wheat farming. One predictable change was the depletion of the soil's nutrients resulting from intensive farming methods of planting and harvesting two wheat crops a year. Unpredictable environmental changes contributing to the slump in wheat production were the problem of wheat rust and chinch bugs. These goals were incorporated with the relevant state and local Geography: People, Places, and Environments social studies standards by providing chances for the fourth graders to:

• Describe and give examples of ways in which people interact with the physical environment, including use of land, location of communities, methods of construction, and design of shelters.

• Identify and distinguish between predictable environmental changes, such as weather patterns and seasons, and unpredictable changes, such as floods and droughts, and describe the social and economic effects of these changes.[42]

Finally, we wanted students to understand some of the economic aspects of wheat and dairy farming, which corresponded to the Production, Distribution, and Consumption[43] national social studies thematic strand. We hoped the fourth graders would learn that one of the motivations for both wheat and dairy farming was farmers' need for income to provide for their basic necessities. When wheat and dairy farming were profitable, farmers continued to produce wheat and milk. When profits decreased, they were less likely to continue this type of farming. The demand for wheat and dairy products within the state, country, and around the world also contributed to the growth of farming. In contrast, we wanted students to understand that competition from wheat production in other states led to the demise of wheat farming in our state in the nineteenth century. Competition from other states' dairy products and from large, corporate farms led to a decline in the number of dairy farms today. Lastly, it was important that students understand some of the processes involved with nineteenth-century wheat farming and contemporary dairy farming in order to appreciate farmers' complex skills, knowledge, and various challenges. These goals matched several Economics: Production, Exchange, and Consumption state and local social studies standards as we offered opportunities for the fourth graders to:

• Identify local goods and services that are part of the global economy and explain their use in Wisconsin.

• Give examples to explain how businesses and industry depend on workers with specialized skills to make production more efficient.

• Identify the economic roles of various institutions, including households, businesses, and government.[44]

SMALL, COOPERATIVE GROUP ACTIVITIES: CULTURALLY RELEVANT BEST TEACHING PRACTICES

In order to provide the best learning opportunities within a limited amount of teaching time, we organized the fourth graders into small, cooperative groups to investigate different aspects of wheat and dairy farming in our state. From our experiences working with the students during previous state history units, we knew small, cooperative group activities engaged more students and resulted in greater learning. We regularly observed the fourth graders constructing knowledge together as they discussed questions, ideas, and problems and investigated photographs, drawings, and artifacts in small groups.[45] Such activities built on the cultural values of cooperation and group achievement[46] and provided additional support for the two English language learners. We were pleased to discover over the course of the semester that a couple of boys from Mexican American and European American backgrounds increased their helping behaviors in small group activities while continuing to be active participants themselves. They assisted Tong, one of the Hmong English language learners, in reading and writing activities, encouraged him to offer his ideas, promoted his participation in group presentations, and quietly coached him during group presentations. They also urged Maria to speak for her group when small groups reported the results of their discussions to the class. Our use of cooperative, small group activities to explore wheat and dairy farming not only built on students' cultural values and provided opportunities for the fourth graders to construct knowledge together, but also followed the recommended best teaching practices in social studies education:

• Use activities that engage students in inquiry and problem solving about significant human issues.

• Form mixed ability groups and have students participate in interactive and cooperative study processes.[47]

Wheat Farming

Because of our limited time, we created a concise summary of wheat farming for students to read. We gave each small group of fourth graders the summary of why wheat farming grew in importance in Wisconsin during the nineteenth century[48] and copies of historically accurate drawings of a Minnesota farm during the 1860s.[49] The drawings illustrated plowing and planting with oxen and later with work horses, growing wheat plants, cutting and gathering wheat by hand and later by machine, threshing by hand and later by machine, and selling wheat. Students also studied photocopies of paintings depicting several farmers cooperatively threshing wheat with a steam-powered tractor in the late 1800s and early 1900s, in the field with a more modern threshing machine during the early 1900s, and a large dinner held by the host farmer for the threshing crew.[50] We asked students to discuss with group members:

1. What would you like about being a wheat farmer in the 1800s?

2. What would you dislike about being a wheat farmer in the 1800s?

3. Why did farmers decide to grow a lot of wheat rather than another crop?

4. Do you think farmers made the right decision to stop growing wheat in the 1880s? Why?

As a means of demonstrating their understanding of wheat farming, small groups prepared dramatizations. We provided written guidelines for each group dramatization:

Wheat Farming Family in Wisconsin in the 1880s

You are a wheat farming family living in Wisconsin in the 1880s. Act out what it was like to be wheat farmers in the 1880s. Show all the work you do, the tools and equipment you use, and the animals which help you. Show how you clear the land, plow the soil, plant wheat, harvest wheat, and take the wheat to flour mills to be made into flour. Show some of the problems you had with growing wheat. Show your decision about whether to continue growing wheat or change to dairy farming in the 1880s.

With our guidance, Hua, Jacob, Carlos, and Tong prepared and presented their dramatization.

Carlos: [to Tong] Come on, go get the oxen, we have to plow the fields [Tong and Carlos "whipped" the oxen and appeared to struggle with guiding the plow back and forth].

Jacob: First farmers used oxen. We have to feed the oxen [Hua and Jacob dramatized feeding oxen by throwing food on the ground].

Hua: Later the farmers used horses [Carlos held "reins" in his hands and walked forward plowing].

Jacob: We have to go feed the horses [Hua and Jacob pantomimed feeding the horses by throwing food on the ground]. Then the farmer brushes the horses [Carlos made motions to suggest brushing horses].

Hua: We have to go cut the wheat [Carlos and Jacob pantomimed cutting and tying wheat into bundles. Tong placed wheat into piles.]

Carlos: [to Jacob] You have to go and get the thresher. We have to thresh the wheat now [Carlos and Tong made hitting motions].

Jacob: Then they have to take it to the flour mill.

Carlos: Okay, we're going to the flour mill now [all four dramatized climbing into a wagon with Carlos driving the wagon and horses].

Carlos: Okay, we're at the flour mill [all four began a relay of lifting bags of wheat from the wagon to pass along to the mill, grimacing from the weight of the bags]. Help me carry this big bag of flour [Jacob and Carlos dramatized carrying a large bag between the two of them to the wagon]. Get in the wagon. Go put the sign out, we're selling the flour.

Tong: [Approached Carlos] I want to buy all your flours [Carlos held out his hand and Tong placed "money" in it. Then Carlos dramatized handing Tong a large bag of flour].

Following the dramatizations, we led a class discussion about what students learned about wheat farming from this activity.

During individual interviews at the close of the unit, we discovered most of the fourth graders understood why Wisconsin farmers began growing wheat, some of the processes involved in wheat farming, its importance in the state, and what led to the decline in wheat farming in the 1880s. Xee described the significance and challenges of wheat farming:

It [wheat] became an important crop because the Civil War was going on. They needed a lot of food to feed the armies. They would have to grow a lot of wheat. Minnesota saw what they [Wisconsin wheat farmers] were doing. They started to grow wheat, too. They said they were going to have a contest to see who grows the most wheat. Wisconsin couldn't grow anymore because of the chinch bugs. They destroyed the crops. They were planting in the same place every year. The soil would get too icky. They couldn't grow anymore. It was really hard. There was planting, harvesting, and keep on going and going until it was done. If you planted a lot of them [wheat], it is hard work.[51]

Neal recognized that wheat farming provided valuable income for farmers until problems with insects, disease, and the soil led to the decline in wheat production:

Wheat was the most important crop in Wisconsin. They got a lot of money for selling it to other states and other people. Pretty soon they started having problems like the chinch bugs were eating crops and rust disease was going around destroying the plants. They started growing so much the ground ran out of nutrients and so they couldn't wheat farm anymore. If you had ten acres that you were growing on, only five acres would grow.[52]

Judy justified the wheat farmers' decision to stop growing wheat:

If I were a wheat farmer, I would stop because it wouldn't make any sense to grow it if it were just going to die.[53]

Dairy Farming

Students remained in their small, cooperative groups to investigate dairy farming. We asked each group of fourth graders to assume the identity of a wheat-farming family living in Wisconsin in the 1880s. Each farm family was experiencing problems in growing enough wheat to earn a living and needed to decide if they should continue to grow wheat or convert to dairy farming. We created a summary of the resources dairy farmers needed, different tasks involved in dairy farming during the late nineteenth century, and changes which occurred in the industry during this period to help each family make a decision.[54] A copy of the summary is shown in Figure 5–4.

A second decision we asked each farm family to make was which breed of dairy cattle they would raise if they chose to become dairy

WHY DID DAIRY FARMING BECOME AN IMPORTANT INDUSTRY IN WISCONSIN?

Name _____ Date _____

You and the others in your group are a family of farmers living in Wisconsin in the 1880s. Now you are wheat farmers, but you are having problems with growing wheat. You are deciding if you should continue to grow wheat or change to dairy farming. Work together to read and discuss the next three pages and the questions. After you have discussed each question, write your idea for each question.

Why did many wheat farmers become dairy farmers?

When wheat farmers in Wisconsin realized they could not grow much wheat in the 1870s, many decided to become dairy farmers. They had to buy good dairy cows, build fences and sheds for their cattle, and grow crops to feed their dairy cattle. They began to grow hay, oats, and corn silage. Farmers discovered the soil in Wisconsin was good for growing these crops. The land made good pastures for cattle to graze. People living in towns in Wisconsin wanted farmers to provide them with the milk, butter, and cheese they needed.

After the late 1880s, farmers began building silos for storing silage for dairy cattle to eat during the winter. Silos were tall towers and may be attached to the barns. Before farmers had silos, they did not have food for dairy cattle to eat during the winter to keep them making milk. If dairy cows do not eat plenty of food, they do not produce milk.

One kind of food farmers made for their dairy cattle was silage. Farmers grew corn, then chopped the corn plants to make silage. The silage was put into the silos. Farmers made another kind of food for dairy cows by grinding corn kernels, corn cobs, oats, and other grains. This was called groundfeed. Still another food was made from hay before it dried, called haylage or wet hay. During the winter dairy farmers fed their cattle all four kinds of food: hay, haylage, silage, and groundfeed. In the summer cows ate alfalfa and grass in pastures. Farmers might also feed their dairy cows green chop or hay that is still green during the summer.

After farmers began feeding their dairy cattle year round, their cows kept producing milk. In 1851, farmers began making cheese. Colby cheese was invented in Wisconsin. Farmers also began taking their milk to creameries or butter factories in the 1870s. Milk with higher butterfat made good butter and farmers were paid according to the amount of butterfat in their milk. Farmers could begin shipping their butter and

194

cheese to other states after refrigerator railroad cars became available in 1871. By 1900, dairy farming had become a big business in Wisconsin.

1. If your family was a wheat farmer in the 1880s, would you have decided to change to dairy farming?

2. Why?

What kinds of dairy cattle did farmers raise?

Dairy farmers raised different breeds of dairy cattle. The most popular breed of dairy cows in Wisconsin is the *Holstein*. Holsteins have a black-and-white coat and are very large. They also give the most milk.

Jerseys have light brown to almost black coloring and a dish-shaped indentation between their eyes. The Jerseys are the smallest dairy cattle. They do not produce as much milk as the Holsteins, but their milk has the highest butterfat. Often families with only one cow owned a Jersey because the cows were easily managed.

The *Guernsey* dairy cattle have a golden brown and white coat. They are a little larger than the Jerseys. Guernseys do not produce as much milk as the Holsteins either, but their milk has more butterfat. Some farmers prefer Guernseys because they eat less food and need less barn space.

The *Brown Swiss* dairy cows have a light brown to dark brown coat. This breed is almost as large as the Holsteins and produce almost as much milk. Milk from this breed is especially good for making cheese. Brown Swiss are popular with farmers who have small farms. Farmers do not have to spend much time caring for this breed of dairy cattle.

The *Ayrshires* have a red-and-white spotted coat or a brown-and-white spotted coat. Ayrshires produce more milk than the Guernseys and Jerseys and almost as much milk as the Holsteins and the Brown Swiss. Their milk has less butterfat than the Guernseys and Jerseys. Farmers who want milk just for their family might have Ayrshires.

3. If your family had chosen to become dairy farmers in the 1880s, what type of dairy cattle would you choose to raise?

4. Why?

Why are there fewer dairy farms in Wisconsin today?

Wisconsin is one of the most important agricultural states in the country. It produced more milk than any other state from 1915 until 1993. Now California produces more milk than Wisconsin. Today it is more difficult for family farmers to make a living from dairy farming unless they

(continues)

have *large* farms of more than five hundred acres and *many* dairy cattle (more than fifty). Farmers found they made less money even though they worked very hard every day. California and other southern states began producing more milk, which competed with the milk produced in Wisconsin. Many family farmers are no longer farming and are getting other jobs. In 1950, there were 143,000 dairy farms in Wisconsin. By 1994, there were only thirty thousand dairy farms left in Wisconsin.

Would you like to be a dairy farmer today?

Dairy farming is very hard work. The women and men of farming families work together to complete all the necessary work. A typical day for a farmer begins around 5:30 a.m. when farmers must milk the cows. In the evening, farmers must milk the cows again. They also feed the dairy cows three times a day to keep them making milk. Cows eat hay, groundfeed, silage, and water. Farmers usually grow the oats, corn, and soybeans which are ground and mixed with salt and minerals to make groundfeed.

Each spring farmers must work the fields. They plow and disk the fields to prepare for spring planting. Farmers then plant such crops as corn, oats, hay, peas, and wheat as food for the dairy cattle. After the crops have been planted, farmers usually have to cultivate their fields to destroy weeds and loosen the soil.

Dairy farmers also must harvest their crops. They may harvest hay green to feed to dairy cows right away during the spring, summer, or fall. Dried hay is also harvested in the summer, but is allowed to dry in the fields before it is baled or made into blocks of hay and stored in barns. Dried hay is fed to cows in the winter. Farmers harvest corn to feed their dairy cattle. They chop the entire plant into silage and store in silos. They also pick cobs of corn and store in corn cribs. Farmers may harvest peas and oats and feed to the dairy cattle right away. Farmers may decide to chop these crops to store in the silo until the winter.

Farmers must clean the places where the animals live. The barnyard must be cleared of manure. Often manure is spread on the fields as fertilizer. Farmers clean calf pens, the milking areas of the barn, areas where cows wait to be milked, and where cows sleep during the winter. The place where the cows are milked must be kept clean. Farmers spray the walls and floors every day to clean them. Clean hay must also be put on the floor of the barn for the cows.

5. Would your family decide to continue dairy farming today?

6. Why?

FIGURE 5–4 Summary of dairy farming for small group discussion

farmers. Our original summary provided brief information on the prevalent breeds of dairy cattle to assist each family in their decision.

Finally, we asked each farm family to decide if they would continue dairy farming today given the hard work and long days, plus the struggle to make a living unless they have a large farm with at least five hundred acres and over fifty dairy cattle. The summary described current challenges for dairy farmers and the many tasks dairy farmers must complete in order to be successful.

In order to provide each farm family with additional background information on dairy farming, we provided picture books for them to review. The texts summarized the history of the dairy industry in Wisconsin, the location of dairy farms in the state, different breeds of dairy cattle, how cows produce milk, how milk is processed for sale, the steps in making cheese from milk, and daily life on a dairy farm.[55] Each family shared their final decisions and rationale for all the questions which allowed all their classmates to hear the different conclusions and the careful reasoning behind each decision.

Following our study of wheat and dairy farming, we asked each family group to dramatize aspects of either wheat or dairy farming to represent their learning (See Figure 5–5). The families who chose to portray dairy farming were given specific guidelines to follow during their dramatizations.

Dairy Farming Family in Wisconsin Today

You are a dairy farming family living in Wisconsin today. Act out what it is like to be dairy farmers today. Show the kind of dairy cattle you raise. Show what it is like to plant, cultivate, and harvest crops to feed the dairy herd. Show how you feed and milk the cows. Show what happens to the milk after it is collected from the cows. Show how you clean the barns and barnyard. Show some of the problems Wisconsin dairy farmers are having today. Show your decision about whether to continue dairy farming or find another job.

Susan, Rameen, and Jake, with some guidance from us, dramatized dairy farmers today.

Rameen: It's 5:30 A.M.

Jake and Susan: We're bringing the cows in.

FIGURE 5–5 Students dramatize the use of milking machines in dairy farming today

Jake: Here, Bossy! [made arm motions as if directing cows into the barn].

Susan: Come on, it's time for milking.

Rameen: We're in the barn now. We're milking cows [all three bent down and pantomimed placing milking machines on several different cows].

Susan: We ran out of machines, so we milk them by hand [bent down and showed milking motions with their hands].

Jake: I'm going to be planting seeds in soil [pantomimed climbing onto a tractor and riding across a field while making "tractor" sounds].

Rameen: I'm putting the seeds in [held onto a "steering wheel" and moved back and forth across the field].

Jake: We're putting crops inside the silo [all three pantomimed shoveling crops].

Rameen: We're putting it into a machine that puts it into the silo.

Rameen: A man from the dairy comes to collect the milk [Jake pantomimed driving to the barn, then backed his truck to the milk storage tank].

Rameen: I'm opening the pipe from the tank [Rameen and Susan dramatized turning the knobs].

Susan: I'm putting it inside [demonstrated connecting the tank to the truck. Jake drove off while Rameen waved him off].

Rameen: And now we're going to clean the barn [all three made sweeping and scooping motions]. We have to put all this stuff on the side [swept to one side while Jake pretended to slip on the debris].

End-of-the-unit interviews showed that the fourth graders understood why many Wisconsin wheat farmers turned to dairy farming in the late 1800s. They recognized that dairy farming produced more income through the sale of milk, butter, and cheese rather than a single wheat product. It was also less expensive because it required fewer acres of land for their dairy cattle than for wheat production. Silos allowed dairy cattle to be fed throughout the winter and kept them producing milk. The soil was more suitable for dairy farming than wheat farming. Charlotte summarized reasons for the change from wheat farming to dairy farming:

> Wheat farmers realized they could make more money in dairy farming than wheat. The bad thing was they couldn't feed them [cows] all year round because they didn't have anything to store food in. Then they thought of the silo. They were able to store food in there. They were able to feed the dairy cows in the winter and keep the milk producing in the winter time. They would get paid more money. Farmers had to order dairy cows from other places because Wisconsin didn't have any dairy cattle before they started.[56]

Rameen suggested the soil as the main reason for the change to dairy farming and recommended the best dairy cattle to raise:

> Wisconsin figured out that the soil was not for wheat. It was for dairy farming. There were cows that you could buy. The best you could have was the Holstein, that made the most milk. I think the best you could buy was the Jersey because it made the most butterfat and they took up less space.[57]

The fourth graders also explained some of the aspects of dairy farming today. They knew dairy farmers had to milk cows twice a day every day; use milking machines and other equipment; grow, harvest, and store different foods for their dairy cattle; test milk for butterfat content; store milk in a refrigerated area; and choose a specific breed of dairy cattle after considering the advantages of each breed. Xee described some of the characteristics and challenges of dairy farming today:

> They would have to wake up so early to milk the cows. They had to milk the cows and they would get more money for that. Now they use machines instead of their hands. If I had a machine, it would take a long time, if you were the only one trying to milk them. You have to go get them [dairy cows]. They wouldn't stay in line. They would be everywhere. You would have to go after them. They [farmers] would be making cheese. Colby cheese was invented in Wisconsin. The Jersey had butterfat in it. If you had a lot of butterfat, you would get more money for it. Butterfat can make butter or cheese. For the black-and-white cows, they use their milk to make cheese sometimes, but usually not. They would give us milk.[58]

Hua concluded that she was not interested in becoming a dairy farmer "Because you have to do a lot of hard stuff, like milk the cows."[59] In contrast, Neal wanted to be a dairy farmer because "You get a lot of money for it and I think it is exciting to have all those cows and milk them."[60]

FOCUS ON YOUR STATE: AGRICULTURE INDUSTRY

In preparation for teaching about the early agriculture industry in your state, you might:

• Contact the state or local historical society for such teaching resources as museum exhibits, historical sites, videos, photographs, websites, trade books and other print documents. Organize the resources to allow students to research the types of farming done during the early history of your state, the different food products produced, and the significance of farming in your state's history.

• Contact your county's agriculture extension agent for background information on early agriculture in your state, its contributions to the economy and quality of life in your state, and its impact on the physical environment.

In preparation for teaching about the current agriculture industry in your state, you could:

• Solicit background information and teaching resources (videos, photographs, websites, trade books, and other print documents) on farming today from your county's agriculture extension agent, local farm collectives, and such farming organizations as the Farm Bureau.

• Identify trade books for your students to read on the type of agriculture which currently exists in your state. Review the annotated list of Notable Social Studies Trade Books for Young People published annually in *Social Education* and the recommended texts described in *Children's Literature in Social Studies: Teaching to the Standards* and *Linking Literature with Life: The NCSS Standards and Children's Literature for the Middle Grades.*[61] Encourage critical literacy by using texts which illustrate how agriculture has benefited and harmed your state.

• Survey your students' families for family members who participate in the agriculture industry today. Invite them to speak to the class about a typical day in the life of a farmer, the tasks farmers must complete, the rewards and challenges of farming, and their perspective on how farming has contributed to and damaged your state. Arrange for a field trip to the farm to see the use of land and other natural resources, buildings, equipment and tools used, animals and crops raised, and some of the farming tasks being completed.

REFLECTIONS AND RECOMMENDATIONS

The strategy of organizing students into small, cooperative groups to investigate, discuss, and make decisions about wheat or dairy farming is not only a recommended best teaching practice,[62] but is very effective with our fourth graders. We encourage you to use a similar strategy with your students to allow them to work together constructing knowledge. We also recommend large group discussions along with small groups, which enable our students to learn enough about dairy and wheat farming that they are able to demonstrate their understandings through their dramatizations. The interviews verify that our students learn from these strategies.

We also highly recommend the use of community resources in studying state industries. They provide rich learning opportunities for our students to understand the lumber and paper industries. Both guest speakers are very knowledgeable about the topic, tell engaging stories about lumbering and paper production, and respond carefully and respectfully to the children's questions. We plan to continue using guest speakers who offer workers' perspectives on an industry, a point of view not often included in the social studies curriculum, and encourage you to identify similar guest speakers. Without such resources, it would be more challenging for our students to understand some of the difficult realities and dangers of work in a lumber camp or lumber mill.

As we continue to improve the curriculum unit, we want to invite guest speakers from the paper industry and dairy farming who could provide workers' perspectives on the daily routines, dangers, and rewards of producing paper or milk. You may also find it valuable for your students to interact with a small, family farmer who could describe the challenges and responsibilities of farming today from the point of view of one who does the work. Someone who currently works in an industry, such as the paper industry, could provide first-hand experiences of daily work within a paper mill, including the benefits and hazards for those who produce paper. Such community resources can provide close-up views of state industries for students, which are difficult to capture in videos or texts.

An area for continual improvement is our use of critical literacy in the study of state industries. We encourage you to make critical literacy an important component of your curriculum. We continue to search for texts which provide different perspectives on industries, including worker and environmental points of view. Elementary students are very capable of considering different perspectives and think about positive and negative aspects of state industries. By studying how industries have harmed the environment or workers, we can prepare students to take action against harmful industrial practices in the future.

ENDNOTES

1. State Historical Society of Wisconsin, *The Days of the Lumberjack: Scenes from the Heyday of Lumbering* (Madison, WI: State Historical Society of Wisconsin, 1965). Each photograph includes an explanatory caption.

2. Chet Kozlak, *Lumberjacks and Logging Coloring Book* (St. Paul, MN: Minnesota Historical Society, 1982), 11–16. Each drawing includes an explanatory caption and the introduction to the coloring book includes background information on logging in Minnesota and Wisconsin.

3. Frederick Risinger, *Trends in K–12 Social Studies* (Eric Digest: ED351278, 1992), 1–5.

4. Christine A. Sleeter and Carl A. Grant, *Making Choices for Multicultural Education: Five Approaches to Race, Class, and Gender*, 3rd ed. (Upper Saddle River, NJ: Merrill, 1999), 188–216.

5. National Council for the Social Studies, *Expectations of Excellence: Curriculum Standards for Social Studies* (Washington, DC: National Council for the Social Studies, 1994), 54–56.

6. Hal Balsiger, Paula DeHart, Margaret A. Laughlin, Stephen A. Rose, and Michael Yell, *Planning Curriculum in Social Studies* (Madison, WI: Wisconsin Department of Public Instruction, 2001), 40.

7. National Council for the Social Studies, 65–66.

8. Balsiger et al., 97.

9. National Council for the Social Studies, 51–53.

10. Karen L. Jorgensen, *History Workshop: Reconstructing the Past with Elementary Students* (Portsmouth, NH: Heinemann, 1993), 13–25.

11. Balsiger et al., 61.

12. William Kurelek, *Lumberjack* (Plattsburgh, NY: Tundra Books, 1974).

13. Jorgensen, 13–25.

14. State Historical Society of Wisconsin; Kozlak, 4–25. For another source which provides authentic drawings and photographs of logging camps, river drives, and sawmills in different parts of the country see Peter Adams, *Early Loggers and the Sawmill* (New York: Crabtree, 1992), 18–62.

15. Kurelek.
16. State Historical Society of Wisconsin.
17. Interview with Carlos, 1/29/98.
18. Interview with Jake, 1/29/98.
19. Interview with Xee, 1/29/98.
20. Interview with Jim, 1/28/98.
21. Interview with Patty, 1/28/98.
22. Interview with Charlotte, 1/29/98.
23. Ibid.
24. Interview with Xee, 1/29/98.
25. DeAn M. Krey, *Children's Literature in Social Studies: Teaching to the Standards* (Washington, DC: National Council for the Social Studies, 1998); Alexa L. Sandmann and John F. Ahern, *Linking Literature with Life: The NCSS Standards and Children's Literature for the Middle Grades* (Washington, DC: National Council for the Social Studies, 2002).
26. Dr. Seuss, *The Lorax* (New York: Random House, 1971).
27. National Council for the Social Studies, 54–56; Balsiger et al., 40.
28. National Council for the Social Studies, 65–66; Balsiger et al., 97.
29. In 2001 Wisconsin Tissue became SCA Tissue, which means Swedish Paper Association, according to recent correspondence with Jeff Johnson. The company has maintained its focus on producing paper products from recycled materials.
30. We later discovered a curriculum unit *Paper Makes Wisconsin Great* designed for grades four and five which contained a videotape, teacher's guide with student activities, fact sheets, sampler of paper-making materials, and a poster showing the steps in making paper. It was created by the Wisconsin Paper Council in July, 1998, and is still available for purchase at $10. Another resource sponsored by the Wisconsin Paper Council is the website "Paper in Wisconsin" located at *www.wipapercouncil.org*. The website includes educator resources, fun facts about the paper industry, different careers in the paper industry, and directions for making paper.
31. Interview with Denise, 1/28/98.
32. Interview with Jim, 1/28/98.
33. Interview with Carlos, 1/29/98.
34. Interview with Susan, 1/28/98.
35. Interview with Patty, 1/28/98.
36. Interview with Carlos, 1/29/98.
37. Krey; Sandmann and Ahern.
38. Lynne Cherry, *A River Ran Wild* (San Diego: Voyager Books, 1992).

39. National Council for the Social Studies, 51–53.
40. Balsiger et al., 61–62.
41. National Council for the Social Studies, 54–56.
42. Balsiger et al., 40.
43. National Council for the Social Studies, 65–66.
44. Balsiger et al., 97.
45. Jere Brophy and Janet Alleman, *Powerful Social Studies for Elementary Students* (New York: Harcourt Brace, 1996), 63–77; Geoffrey Scheurman, "From Behaviorist to Constructivist Teaching," *Social Education* 62 (1998), 6–9.
46. Carrie Rothstein-Fisch, Patricia M. Greenfield, and Elise Trumball, "Bridging Cultures with Classroom Strategies," *Educational Leadership* 56 (1999), 64–67.
47. Steven Zemelman, Harvey Daniels, and Arthur Hyde, *Best Practice: New Standards for Teaching and Learning in America's Schools* (Portsmouth, NH: Heinemann, 1998), 132–155.
48. The summary was based on an article about wheat farming in a state history magazine written for fourth graders, *Badger History*. Richard Powers, "Wheat is King!" *Badger History* 30 (1977), 4–10.
49. Mary Ellen Schultz, *The Kelley Farm Activity Book* (St. Paul, MN: Minnesota Historical Society, 1985), 4–9, 14, 16–20.
50. Chester Garthwaite, *Threshing Days: The Farm Paintings by Lavern Kammerude* (Mount Horeb, WI: Wisconsin Folk Museum, 1990), 42–52.
51. Interview with Xee, 1/29/98.
52. Interview with Neal, 1/29/98.
53. Interview with Judy, 1/30/98.
54. The summary was based primarily on articles about dairy farming in *Badger History*, a state history magazine for fourth graders. Howard Kanetzke, "Becoming America's Dairyland," *Badger History* 30 (1977), 34–44; Howard Kanetzke, "America's Dairyland," *Badger History* 24 (1971), 5–15; Marguerite Van Hulst, "Dairy Cows," *Badger History* 24 (1971), 18–25; Lynn Kraemer, "Wisconsin is the Home of Colby Cheese," *Badger History* 24 (1971), 46–51; "Families Opt Out of Farming: Medium-Sized Farms Decreasing the Most in State," *Oshkosh Northwestern* (July 11, 1994).
55. The following texts provide valuable background information on dairy farming. Cris Peterson, *Century Farm: 100 Years on a Family Farm* (Honesdale, PA: Boyds Mills, 1999); Cris Peterson, *Extra Cheese, Please! Mozzarella's Journey from Cow to Pizza* (Honesdale, PA: Boyds Mills, 1994); Vincent Scuro, *Wonders of Dairy Cattle* (New York: Dodd,

Mead, 1986); Lynn M. Stone, *Dairy Country* (Vero Beach, FL: Rourke, 1993); Donald Carrick, *Milk* (New York: Greenwillow, 1985); Sandra Ziegler, *A Visit to the Dairy Farm* (Chicago: Childrens Press, 1987); Gail Gibbons, *The Milk Makers* (New York: Macmillan, 1985).
56. Interview with Charlotte, 1/29/98.
57. Interview with Rameen, 1/30/98.
58. Interview with Xee, 1/29/98.
59. Interview with Hua, 1/28/98.
60. Interview with Neal, 1/29/98.
61. Krey; Sandmann and Ahern.
62. Zemelman et al., 132–155.

CHAPTER 6

TEACHING FOR LEARNING, LEARNING FROM TEACHING

Our journey to teach a multicultural state history curriculum included the goal of encouraging our students to value their own culture and those of many different groups in our state. On the day we concluded teaching about the history of Wisconsin, we witnessed some evidence of meeting this goal. Xee, one of our four Hmong students, surprised us with a special presentation of a traditional Hmong dance and food. She had secretly worked with the school's ESL teacher and interpreter in practicing the dance with other Hmong children and arranging for traditional Hmong foods to be brought to our classroom. Xee seemed to understand that we and the class valued her Hmong cultural background and would enjoy viewing a Hmong dance and eating egg rolls, sticky rice, and "Hmong rice." The class watched in appreciation as Xee and her friends completed the dance and explained different pieces of their Hmong New Year outfits. Everyone especially enjoyed sampling some of the different Hmong foods, especially the delicious egg rolls which Xee and her mother made. Through our state history curriculum, all students learned more about Hmong history and culture as part of our state's history and developed some appreciation for the contributions Hmong people made to our state. Xee's special presentation on Hmong culture was a sign that we made progress in our journey.

This text has described our efforts to provide elementary students with rich learning opportunities through a state history curriculum which integrated multicultural ideas, standards, critical literacy, social constructivist pedagogy, culturally relevant teaching methods, and best teaching practices for social studies. We not only looked for evidence of student learning, but also how we might improve our teaching. At different points along the journey we plan, teach, reflect on, analyze, and evaluate our teaching and what students are learning, then consider modifications in our teaching. Not only do we want students to learn important multicultural concepts and main ideas about state history, but we continue to discover the most effective strategies for learning. We offer the main insights we have gained from our experiences in teaching multicultural state history to assist you in enriching your own teaching.

1. FOCUS ON MULTICULTURAL IDEAS WHILE ADDRESSING SOCIAL STUDIES STANDARDS IN YOUR STATE HISTORY CURRICULUM

Multicultural Content

Our primary concern is to teach a multicultural state history curriculum because this approach, we believe, is one way to study examples of inequalities in times past in preparation for creating a more fair, just world for the future. Most elementary students are capable of learning from such an orientation and will become more involved and more likely to learn than if state history is presented as an inevitable sequence of events and facts. Teaching different cultures, including the students' cultural backgrounds, is a best teaching practice,[1] because it offers avenues for students to make personal connections with the curriculum and become actively engaged in learning. We encourage you, too, to provide opportunities for your students to:

• Study different cultures that exist in your state, including your students' own families' cultural backgrounds.

• Examine the issues of racism, sexism, and classism in state industries and voting rights struggles in your state and across the country.

• Study the process of becoming a state through the experiences and perspectives of women and men from different cultural and socio-economic groups.

• Critically analyze different points of view on the fur trade, treaties, treaty rights, removal of Native people to reservations and Native children's forced attendance at boarding schools in your state.

• Consider actions to take to counter prejudice and discrimination that Native Americans or other groups currently face in your state.

Although our fourth graders, like most elementary students, were significantly challenged by these multicultural ideas, they responded with a strong sense of justice and fairness. We regularly heard, "That's not fair!" as students learned about European immigrants who faced humiliating health inspections at Ellis Island and Native American nations who struggled to hold onto their homelands.

We encourage you to regularly review the multicultural content of your state history curriculum to identify areas for improvement. As we reflect on the multicultural ideas in our units, we recognize there are several additions that would make our curriculum even more effective. For example, we want to include Native American nations in the study of family history and the different cultural groups that make up our state to emphasize Native people were the first residents. Elders from different nations should be invited as guest speakers to provide authentic sources for Native American culture and history and Native people's perspectives on the history of our state. In our investigation of state industries, we want to include the Menominee's lumbering business as an example of a Native American nation which followed a sustainable yield policy. Unlike most European American lumber companies which clear-cut forested areas in the nineteenth century, the Menominee replanted trees as they harvested lumber, a practice they continue today. We also recognize the importance of including worker and environmental perspectives on each state industry to illustrate different points of view on the effects of industry on workers and the environment.

Multicultural Resources

Acknowledging the challenges of developing and teaching a multicultural state history curriculum, we suggest additional resources which you may find helpful, including this text. You may want to review Ava's website for five Wisconsin history resource units. Even though the curriculum units focus on Wisconsin, a number of the resources and activities could be used in teaching the history of many different states. The website is available at *www.socialstudies.esmartweb.com.* Two excellent texts which contain examples of multicultural lesson plans and classroom activities in different subject areas are *Turning on Learning: Five Approaches for Multicultural Teaching Plans for Race, Class, Gender, and Disability*[2] and *Beyond Heroes and Holidays: A Practical Guide to K–12 Anti-Racist, Multicultural Education and Staff Development.*[3] In addition, your local and state historical societies, museums, Native American nations, immigrant and refugee organizations may have valuable teaching resources.

Social Studies Standards

Although a multicultural approach to state history is an important impetus for our project, we also recognize the necessity of addressing national, state, and local social studies standards. Thelma's school district expects teachers to teach the standards in each subject. You, like most teachers, face similar expectations. Fortunately, there are many areas of compatibility between the standards and significant multicultural concepts and themes. You may want to first focus on important multicultural ideas, then identify the corresponding standards for your state history curriculum. Or, you may want to begin with the standards, and transform them with a multicultural approach. For example, one of the broad themes from the national standards, the Time, Continuity, and Change thematic strand, includes the specific performance standard that students will "demonstrate an understanding that different people may describe the same event or situation in diverse ways, citing reasons for the different views."[4] However, you can include the perspectives of women and men from various cultures and social classes about a significant event or trend in your state history. The inclusion of diverse group experiences and perspectives is an important aspect of a multicultural curriculum. By integrating the standard with a multicultural approach, you have stronger support for your multicultural state history curriculum.

2. INTEGRATE LITERACY AND CRITICAL LITERACY IN YOUR STATE HISTORY CURRICULUM

We highly recommend the integration of literacy and critical literacy with your state history curriculum. Not only is it a best teaching practice to integrate social studies with other areas of the curriculum,[5] but we have observed benefits for our students. It provides more instructional time for social studies when we, as many teachers, struggle to find the time necessary to devote to an in-depth state history curriculum. Our students have more learning opportunities when they examine important social studies concepts and ideas during reading and language arts as well as social studies, as shown in Figure 6–1. Some children learn best through reading and writing activities. In fact, a number of our fourth graders claimed they learned the most state history content from reading and discussing a text.

FIGURE 6–1 Thelma guides students in thinking critically about their reading

We discovered that critical literacy is more challenging to integrate with state history because we must:

- Monitor who talks in discussions and who is silent.

- Use texts which raise social issues or issues of inequality.

- Raise such issues in discussions when texts or students neglect them.

- Encourage students to make personal connections with—but question—what they read.[6]

Monitor Discussions

We recommend developing strategies to encourage more quiet students to participate in discussions, but also make everyone in the class aware of the significance of asserting one's power through speaking. As we carefully monitored small group discussions, we encouraged the reticent students to speak, affirmed their ideas, and asked them to report on the results of their small group discussion to the whole class. We also asked everyone to observe who was making contributions to discussions and to solicit ideas from less talkative students. Although some students continued to dominate class discussions, a few became more solicitous of others' contributions. We were especially pleased to observe such a change in two boys who tended to assert their views frequently.

Select Appropriate Texts

Although it can be difficult to identify texts which raise social issues or provide authentic representations of different cultures, we were pleased with the reliable texts we used to teach about Native American culture and history and voting rights in our state. An area we want to improve is using trade books which provide worker and/or environmental perspectives on state industries or raise questions about worker rights and environmental impact. We have identified several sources for suggestions of good trade books addressing such issues as sexism and racism and portraying diverse cultures accurately. In each issue of *Rethinking Schools,* a publication for educators concerned about improving schools, is a description of recommended teaching resources, including trade books. More information is available through its website *www.rethinkingschools.org. Teaching Tolerance*, a magazine for educators available free of charge, usually describes teaching resources for addressing different social issues and diverse cultures. Consult the website, *www.teachingtolerance.org,* for additional background on the magazine and teaching ideas and resources. The free catalog "Teaching for Change" offers multicultural books for purchase and can be obtained by phone, (800) 763–9131 or email at *necadc@aol.com.* Oyate also has an online catalog of authentic trade books for teaching about Native American nations and can be accessed through *www.oyate.org.*

Encourage Questions

Another challenge of integrating critical literacy with state history is encouraging students to question what they read and the fairness of specific actions or events described in texts. However, we believe our fourth graders think more deeply about their reading when they do so. Even struggling readers offer ideas on what is right or fair for specific groups described in trade books. Our discussions are richer in content when we not only focus on summarizing main ideas, but also questioning why events resulted in specific outcomes and their fairness for different cultural groups in our state's history.

On occasion, the students develop a questioning attitude which exceeds our expectations. Toward the end of our state history curriculum, Susan spoke with us about a special dramatization she and Judy were planning to present to the class to demonstrate all they were learning. Susan explained that their "play" was going to show that "kids should be able to vote because we can read." Our discussions and texts portraying state and national voting rights activists who advocated for equal opportunities for women and African Americans apparently struck a chord with Susan and Judy. They planned to champion for voting rights for kids. Just as we encouraged the fourth graders to question the fairness of denying voting rights to women and African Americans after Wisconsin became a state, Susan questioned why children could not also have these rights.

3. USE SMALL, COOPERATIVE GROUP ACTIVITIES IN YOUR STATE HISTORY CURRICULUM

We strongly recommend the use of small, cooperative group activities as your students study state history. If each group includes girls and boys from different achievement levels, various social classes, and diverse cultural backgrounds, the composition of the groups is enriched and students learn about each other and how to work with class members they might not choose to work with on their own. At the beginning of each state history unit, we created new groups so students had opportunities to work with everyone else in the class at some point during the curriculum. Forming mixed ability groups and having students participate in interactive and cooperative study processes is a best teaching practice[7] because it provides more opportunities for students to be engaged, teach one another, and construct knowledge together.[8] Among our students, more claimed to learn state history content from small group activities, especially cooperative research, than any other teaching strategy.

However, you need to be prepared to spend additional time teaching your students how to work together cooperatively, monitoring everyone's participation, and guiding students in evaluating their progress in working well as a group. We believe this is time well spent. In our experiences, small group activities allow elementary students to accomplish difficult tasks in a history workshop,[9] complete small group research of different cultural groups or Native American nations, or finish family group investigations into the effects of becoming a state on their "family" or their family's decision to become dairy farmers or remain wheat farmers. Small groups provide a structure to help English-language learners be involved and learn, especially if they can speak in their first language with more proficient English speakers. We also discovered we can more easily assist children with academic tasks and encourage everyone to offer and accept help in small groups. A closer classroom community seems to be created through regular small group activities in our state history curriculum. We witnessed this as Carlos, Neal, and Maria worked together during the unit on becoming a state and voting rights. Because Maria was more quiet, we often encouraged her to participate in small and large group discussions. When Maria struggled to report the results of her small group discussion to the class, Carlos and Neal silently cheered her on.

While small group activities are valuable to include in your state history curriculum, they should be balanced with individual and whole class activities to accommodate students' different learning styles and family preferences. A few fourth graders complained about our requirement to work cooperatively with others and preferred to work alone. During conferences with two European American families, parents criticized the prevalence of small group activities in our state history curriculum. They were worried that their children's learning was hindered by spending time helping others in their group and appeared more concerned about their child's individual achievement over cooperation with others for everyone's achievement. In contrast, several families, especially Hmong parents, were pleased to hear about their child's helping behaviors in small groups. Although we explained the social and academic benefits of cooperative activities to the students and their families and continued such activities throughout the state history curriculum, we also asked students to complete some tasks individually to accommodate student and family preferences.

4. INCLUDE FAMILY AND COMMUNITY RESOURCES IN YOUR STATE HISTORY CURRICULUM

For a richer state history curriculum, we strongly encourage you to integrate local resources, especially from your families and community. Family members may have knowledge difficult to find in other sources and integrating family guest speakers communicates a respect for this knowledge. When family members describe the benefits and challenges of immigrating to the state, the effects of European American settlement on their Native nation's homelands, or their experiences as workers in different state industries, your students will more likely make personal connections to state history and learn important ideas from the stories. When Rameen's mother described her family's motivations for leaving India and settling in Wisconsin, the students were very attentive and asked good questions. They heard a personal story of Rameen's family's desire for better educational opportunities for their children, even if it meant leaving a successful business behind in India and struggling to learn English and finding jobs in Wisconsin. Including family guest speakers also makes your state history curriculum multicultural when families describe different cultural perspectives and experiences in the history of your state. All students may benefit from family guest speakers, who are often more engaging than some texts, Internet sources, or videos.

An area we hope to improve is involving more family and community resources in our state history curriculum, especially as guest speakers. The guest speakers we included on family history and state industries were excellent. They were very knowledgeable, explained important ideas in language children could understand, and responded clearly to the students' questions. In the future, we want to involve family and community guest speakers to provide worker and environmental perspectives on state industries and Native American perspectives on the history and culture of their own nations as well as on different events in state history.

Including guest speakers is also a culturally relevant teaching method for several children, which can provide greater learning opportunities.[10] For some families, their cultural backgrounds include strong oral traditions for passing along history and culture to the next generation. This is especially true for Native American and Hmong families in which elders or adults tell stories communicating important historical events and cultural values. When these oral traditions are brought into the curriculum, you not only are welcoming these cultures into the classroom, but Native American and Hmong students' learning may be enhanced because the state history curriculum includes their home culture. In addition, students from various cultures are introduced to these cultural traditions through such guest speakers.

5. COLLABORATE WITH AT LEAST ONE OTHER TEACHER IN ENRICHING YOUR STATE HISTORY CURRICULUM

To meet the challenges of developing and teaching a multicultural state history curriculum, we especially recommend collaboration with at least one other teacher with similar goals. This educator might be someone at your school, at another school, or a university. Through working with another teacher, you have twice the teaching resources, experiences, and strategies upon which to draw (illustrated in Figure 6–2). You may divide some of the work involved in gathering resources, deciding on appropriate teaching strategies, and creating curriculum. If you are able to collaborate with another educator at your school, or at a nearby school or university, you may easily share such teaching resources as artifacts, photographs, trade books, guest speakers, field trips, simulations, and videos. However, it is always

FIGURE 6–2 Ava and Thelma review resources for teaching Wisconsin history

possible to discuss by phone or email plans for your state history curriculum, what your students are learning from your teaching, and successes and challenges you face in teaching a multicultural state history curriculum. Collaborating allows you to talk over your teaching experiences with another interested, supportive teacher. You may share activities that go well and those which do not lead to student learning, resources which help teach important ideas or concepts and those which do not.

We recognize the benefits of collaboration in our own project. Each of us has expertise in different areas of state history and literacy curricula, access to various resources, and experience with diverse teaching strategies. However, we both are committed to the goal of providing rich learning opportunities for all our students, respecting and building on the children's backgrounds in the classroom, making connections between the curriculum and students' families, and teaching about different cultural groups.

We are fortunate to have many resources upon which to draw, even as we recognize the need for additional materials for some components of our state history curriculum. Thelma contributes resources from her own professional library, her school, and the school district while Ava collects resources from the state historical society, the department of public instruction, the university's educational materials collection, and her own professional library. Thelma's teaching expertise is based on many years of experience teaching Wisconsin history and literacy and the inclusion of class discussions, projects, reports, and plays as avenues for students to learn and demonstrate their knowledge. Prior to this project, Ava had not taught Wisconsin history, but had completed research on Native American and Hmong culture and history in the state, regularly used small, cooperative groups, and developed instructional activities using trade books, artifacts, and photographs in her social studies methods course. Thelma is familiar with the school district's expectations for literacy and Wisconsin history curricula and can decide what is important to teach while Ava is aware of national standards, recommendations for best teaching practices for social studies, and a multicultural social studies curriculum. By pooling our resources, experiences, and knowledge of state history content and standards, we created a much richer Wisconsin history curriculum than either of us could have prepared alone.

6. REFLECT ON, EVALUATE, AND IMPROVE YOUR STATE HISTORY TEACHING

Finally, we encourage you to take time to reflect or think deeply about your teaching and students' learning of your state history curriculum. With the many demands of classroom teaching, teachers often have little thinking time. However, by taking time before or after school, while traveling between your home and school, during the evenings, or on weekends to reflect on teaching your state history curriculum, you can make changes to clearly address your goals and provide greater learning opportunities for your students. If you want a more detailed account of specific lessons or activities, you might ask someone to videotape your teaching. You may then review the videotape for important ideas that you emphasized and students' responses and learning. Collaborating with another educator in developing state history curriculum provides another person to talk with regarding your lessons, what students are learning, difficulties you are experiencing, and what is going well. As you reflect on your teaching, you might consider:

• What are the important multicultural ideas and concepts about state history I want to teach?

• How do I know I am teaching these significant ideas and concepts?

• What multicultural ideas and concepts are my students learning?

• How do I know that students are learning these ideas and concepts?

• What are students having difficulty learning? Why?

• What teaching strategies have been most effective in promoting student learning? Why?

As we collaboratively taught our Wisconsin history curriculum, we set aside a day once a month to reflect and plan. These times were very important in analyzing and evaluating our teaching and student engagement and learning. They were opportunities to step away from the hectic pace of classroom teaching, meet at one of our homes, and to think more deeply about specific teaching activities and students' responses. Jointly, we pooled our insights about the students, their learning, and the effectiveness of our teaching. For example, during one of these sessions, we discussed the effectiveness of the Ellis Island simulation in engaging students actively in thinking about what it was like for European immigrants to enter the United States and planned to use additional simulations in later lessons. During one of our later "reflect-and-plan" days, we talked over our puzzlement regarding the outcome of the vote for statehood simulation and concluded we did not provide enough discussion time for students to explain the reasons for their vote and what they learned from the simulation.

By taking time to reflect on our teaching, we also noted fourth graders who had difficulties working in small groups or appeared uninvolved in whole class activities. We considered how we might improve our teaching by brainstorming additional teaching strategies for engaging all students in whole class discussions and small group activities. During these reflective deliberations, we recognized when we posed questions to the whole class, typically the most assertive, confident students responded. Future lessons included more small group discussions to allow students to discuss questions with a few others, gain confidence in their responses, then offer their answers to the whole class. We also carefully monitored small groups to encourage quiet students to participate, verify their understanding of main points, affirm their contributions, and report the results of the small group discussion to the full class.

Although our journey to teach a multicultural state history curriculum is not yet over, we and our fourth graders traveled far and enjoyed rich experiences along the route. Students learned about the history of our state and we learned more about teaching to meet our multicultural goals. We hope the experiences described within this text encourage you to begin or inspire you to continue your own journey.

ENDNOTES

1. Steven Zemelman, Harvey Daniels, and Arthur Hyde, *Best Practice: New Standards for Teaching and Learning in America's Schools* (Portsmouth, NH: Heinemann, 1998), 132–155.
2. Carl A. Grant and Christine E. Sleeter, *Turning on Learning: Five Approaches for Multicultural Teaching Plans for Race, Class, Gender, and Disability*, 2nd ed. (Upper Saddle River, NJ: Merrill, 1998).
3. Enid Lee, Deborah Menkart, and Margo Okazawa-Rey, eds., *Beyond Heroes and Holidays: A Practical Guide to K–12 Anti-Racist, Multicultural Education and Staff Development* (Washington, DC: Network of Educators on the Americas, 1998).
4. National Council for the Social Studies, *Expectations of Excellence: Curriculum Standards for Social Studies* (Washington, DC: National Council for the Social Studies, 1994), 51.
5. Steven Zemelman, Harvey Daniels, and Arthur Hyde, *Best Practice: New Standards for Teaching and Learning in America's Schools* (Portsmouth, NH: Heinemann, 1998), 132–155.
6. Donna C. Creighton, "Critical Literacy in the Elementary Classroom," *Language Arts* 74 (1997), 438–445; Carole Edelsky, "Education for Democracy," in JoBeth Allen, ed., *Class Actions: Teaching for Social Justice in Elementary and Middle School* (New York: Teachers College Press, 1999), 147–156.
7. Zemelman, et al., 132–155.
8. Jere Brophy and Janet Alleman, *Powerful Social Studies for Elementary Students* (New York: Harcourt Brace, 1996), 63–77; Geoffrey Scheurman, "From Behaviorist to Constructivist Teaching," *Social Education* 62 (1998), 6–9.
9. Karen L. Jorgensen, *History Workshop: Reconstructing the Past with Elementary Students* (Portsmouth, NH: Heinemann, 1993), 13–25.
10. Gloria Ladson-Billings, "But That's Just Good Teaching! The Case for Culturally Relevant Pedagogy," *Theory Into Practice* 34 (1995), 159–165; Valerie O. Pang and Robertta H. Barba, "The Power of Culture: Building Culturally Affirming Instruction," in Carl A. Grant, ed., *Educating for Diversity: An Anthology of Multicultural Voices* (Boston: Allyn and Bacon, 1995), 341–358.

BIBLIOGRAPHY

Adams, Peter. 1992. *Early Loggers and the Sawmill.* New York: Crabtree.

Adler, David A. 1994. *A Picture Book of Sojourner Truth.* New York: Holiday House.

Airasian, Peter W. and Mary E. Walsh. 1997. "Constructivist Cautions." *Phi Delta Kappan* 78 (February): 444–449.

American Indian Language and Culture Education Board. n.d. *The History of the Hochungra People: Winnebago Tribe of Wisconsin.* Madison, WI. American Indian Language and Culture Education Board.

Association of American Geographers and National Council for Geographic Education. 1984. *Guidelines for Geographic Education: Elementary and Secondary Schools.* Washington, DC: Association of American Geographers.

Balsiger, Hal, Paula DeHart, Margret A. Laughlin, Stephen A. Rose and Michael Yell. 2001. *Planning Curriculum in Social Studies.* Madison, WI: Wisconsin Department of Public Instruction.

Belcher-Hamilton, Lisa. 1989. "The Underground Railroad: The Beginning of Douglass's Journey." *Cobblestone* 10 (February): 15–17.

———. 1988. "The League of Women Voters." *Cobblestone* 9 (November): 35–36.

Berman, Sheldon. 1990. "Educating for Social Responsibility." *Educational Leadership* 48 (November): 75–80.

Bohn, Anita P. and Christine E. Sleeter. 2000. "Multicultural Education and the Standards Movement: A Report from the Field." *Phi Delta Kappan* 82 (October): 156–159.

Brophy, Jere and Janet Alleman. 1996. *Powerful Social Studies for Elementary Students*. New York: Harcourt Brace.

Brown, Victoria. 1975. *Uncommon Lives of Common Women: The Missing Half of Wisconsin History*. Madison, WI: Wisconsin Feminists Project Fund.

Bunting, Eve. 1995. *Cheyenne Again*. New York: Clarion.

Cain, Becky. 1995. "Learning from the Suffragists: The League of Women Voters Educates Citizens for Action." *Social Education* 59 (September): 290–292.

Carrick, Donald. 1985. *Milk*. New York: Greenwillow.

Cha, Dia. 1996. *Dia's Story Cloth*. New York: Lee & Low.

Cherry, Lynne. 1992. *A River Ran Wild*. San Diego, CA: Voyager Books.

Clark, James I. 1956. *Wisconsin Women Fight for Suffrage*. Madison, WI: The State Historical Society of Wisconsin.

Cohen, Elizabeth G. 1998. "Making Cooperative Learning Equitable." *Educational Leadership* 56 (September): 18–21.

Connell, Kate. 1993. *They Shall Be Heard: Susan B. Anthony & Elizabeth Cady Stanton*. Austin, TX: Raintree Steck-Vaughn.

Creighton, Donna C. 1997. "Critical Literacy in the Elementary Classroom." *Language Arts* 74 (October): 438–445.

Demos, John. 1995. *The Tried and the True: Native American Women Confronting Colonization*. New York: Oxford University Press.

Douglass, Frederick. 1989. "The ABC's." *Cobblestone* 10 (February): 11–14.

Dr. Seuss. 1971. *The Lorax*. New York: Random House.

Duvall, Jill. 1991. *The Oneida*. Chicago: Childrens Press.

Edelsky, Carole. 1999. "Education for Democracy." In *Class Actions: Teaching for Social Justice in Elementary and Middle School*, edited by JoBeth Allen, 147–156. New York: Teachers College Press.

———. 1999. "On Critical Whole Language Practice: Why, What, and a Bit of How." In *Making Justice Our Project: Teachers Working Toward Critical Whole Language Practice*, edited by Carole Edelsky, 19–36. Urbana, IL: National Council of Teachers of English.

English, Billie Joan and Sharon Cooper Calhoun. 1987. *The Wisconsin Story*. Oklahoma City, OK: Apple Corps.

Erickson, Sue. 1994. *Chippewa Treaties: Understanding and Impact, 2nd ed.* Odanah, WI: Great Lakes Indian Fish and Wildlife Commission.

Feldman, Ruth Tenzer. 1998. "The Dredful Scott Decision." *Cobblestone* 19 (October): 26–30.

Ferris, Jeri. 1988. *Walking the Road to Freedom: A Story About Sojourner Truth*. Minneapolis, MN: Carolrhoda Books.

Fishel, Leslie H. 1963. "Wisconsin and Negro Suffrage." *Wisconsin Magazine of History* 46 (Spring): 180–196.

Fridley, Russell W. and Jean A Brookins. 1982. *Where the Two Worlds Meet: The Great Lakes Fur Trade*. St. Paul, MN: Minnesota Historical Society.

Fritz, Jean. 1995. *You Want Women to Vote, Lizzie Stanton?* New York: G. P. Putnam's Sons.

Gard, Carolyn. 1996. "Elections in the Colonies." *Cobblestone* 17 (October): 4–9.

Garthwaite, Chester. 1990. *Threshing Days: The Farm Paintings by Lavern Kammerude*. Mount Horeb, WI: Wisconsin Folk Museum.

Gehret, Jeanne. 1994. *Susan B. Anthony: And Justice for All.* Fairport, NY: Verbal Images Press.

Gibbons, Gail. 1985. *The Milk Makers*. New York: Macmillan.

Gold, Susan Dudley. 1997. *Indian Treaties*. New York: Twenty-First Century Books.

Grant, Carl A. and Christine E. Sleeten. 1998. *Turning on Learning: Five Approaches for Multicultural Teaching Plans for Race, Class, Gender, and Disability, 2nd ed.* Upper Saddle River, NJ: Merrill.

Greene, Meg. 1998. "The Best System We Could Get." *Cobblestone* 19 (October): 4–7.

Harvey, Karen D, Lisa D. Harjo, and Jane K. Jackson. 1997. *Teaching About Native Americans, 2nd ed.* Washington, DC: National Council for the Social Studies.

Harvey, Karen D, Lisa D. Harjo, and Lynda Welborn. 1995. *How to Teach About American Indians: A Guide for the School Library Media Specialist*. Westport, CT: Greenwood Press.

Hieb, Jane A. 1994. *Visions and Voices: Winnebago Elders Speak to the Children*. Independence, WI: Western Dairyland Economic Opportunity Council.

Hirschfelder, Arlene and Yvonne Beamer. 2000. *Native Americans Today: Resources and Activities for Educators Grades 4–8*. Englewood, CO: Teacher Ideas Press.

Hong, Karen E. 1989. "Fredrick Douglass and Women's Rights." *Cobblestone* 10 (February): 25–28.

Hunter, Sally M. 1997. *Four Seasons of Corn: A Winnebago Tradition*. Minneapolis, MN: Lerner.

Johnson, Delores. 1993. *Now Let Me Fly: The Story of a Slave Family*. New York: Macmillan.

Jorgensen, Karen L. 1993. *History Workshop: Reconstructing the Past with Elementary Students*. Portsmouth, NH: Heinemann.

Kalbacken, Joan. 1994. *The Menominee*. Chicago: Childrens Press.

Kanetzke, Howard W. 1971. "America's Dairyland." *Badger History* 24 (January): 5–15.

———. 1973. "The Wisconsin Territory." *Badger History* 27 (September): 4–25.

———. 1975. "From Northwest Ordinance to Statehood." *Badger History* 29 (September): 52–57.

———. 1976. "Oshkosh and Menominee Lands." *Badger History* 29 (March): 56–60.

———. 1976. "Wa Kun Cha Koo Kah, Yellow Thunder." *Badger History* 29 (March): 61–64.

———. 1977. "Becoming America's Dairyland." *Badger History* 30 (March): 34–44.

———. 1978. "Wisconsin's Constitution." *Badger History* 32 (November): 4–9.

King, Sandra. 1993. *Shannon: An Ojibway Dancer*. Minneapolis, MN: Lerner.

Kozlak, Chet. 1979. *Ojibway Indians Coloring Book*. St. Paul, MN: Minnesota Historical Society.

———. 1981. *A Great Lakes Fur Trade Coloring Book*. St. Paul, MN: Minnesota Historical Society.

———. 1982. *Lumberjacks and Logging Coloring Book*. St. Paul, MN: Minnesota Historical Society.

Kraemer, Lynn. 1971. "Wisconsin is the Home of Colby Cheese." *Badger History* 24 (January): 46–51.

Krass, Peter. 1988. *Sojourner Truth: Antislavery Activist*. New York: Chelsea House.

Krey, DeAn M. 1998. *Children's Literature in Social Studies: Teaching to the Standards*. Washington, DC: National Council for the Social Studies.

Kroll, Steven. 1995. *Ellis Island: Doorway to Freedom*. New York: Holiday House.

Krull, Kathleen. 1995. *One Nation, Many Tribes: How Kids Live in Milwaukee's Indian Community*. New York: Lodestar Books.

Kurelek, William. 1974. *Lumberjack*. Plattsburgh, NY: Tundra Books.

Kusek, Karen H. 1989. "Frederick Douglass, Abolitionist Writer." *Cobblestone* 10 (February): 21–24.

Ladson-Billings, Gloria. 1995. "But That's Just Good Teaching! The Case for Culturally Relevant Pedagogy." *Theory Into Practice* 34 (Summer): 159–165.

Lankiewicz, Donald. 1983. "The Immigration Station." *Cobblestone* 4 (January): 6–9.

Lawrence, Jacob. 1993. *The Great Migration: An American Story*. New York: HarperCollins.

Lee, Enid, Deborah Menkart, and Margo Okazawa-Rey, eds. 1998. *Beyond Heroes and Holidays: A Practical Guide to K–12 Anti-Racist, Multicultural Education and Staff Development*. Washington, DC: Networks of Educators on the Americas.

Levine, Ellen. 1993. *If Your Name Was Changed at Ellis Island*. New York: Scholastic.

Lucas, Eileen. 1994. *The Ojibwas: People of the Northern Forests*. Brookfield, CT: Millbrook.

Mack, Jay, Paul Dekock, and Dave Yount. 1993. *Gateway: A Simulation of Immigration Issues in Past and Present America*. Carlsbad, CA: Interact.

Maestro, Betsy. 1996. *Coming to America: The Story of Immigration*. New York: Scholastic.

Matthaei, Gay, and Jewel H. Grutman. 1994. *The Ledgerbook of Thomas Blue Eagle*. New York: Lickle.

McCully, Emily Arnold. 1996. *The Ballot Box Battle*. New York: Alfred A. Knopf.

McCurdy, Michael, ed. 1994. *Escape from Slavery: The Boyhood of Frederick Douglass in His Own Words*. New York: Alfred A. Knopf.

McKissack, Patricia C. and Frederick McKissack. 1992. *Sojourner Truth: Ain't I a Woman?* New York: Scholastic.

McLellan, Joe. 1991. *Nanabosho Dances*. Winnipeg, Canada: Pemmican Publications.

Miller, William. 1995. *Frederick Douglass: The Last Day of Slavery*. New York: Lee & Low Books.

National Council for the Social Studies. 1994. *Expectations of Excellence: Curriculum Standards for Social Studies*. Washington, DC: National Council for the Social Studies.

Olneck, Michael. 2000. "Can Multicultural Education Change What Counts as Cultural Capital?" *American Educational Research Journal* 37 (Summer): 317–348.

Ortiz, Simon. 1988. *The People Shall Continue*. San Francisco, CA: Children's Book Press.

Oshkosh Northwestern. 1994. "Families Opt Out of Farming: Medium-Sized Farms Decreasing the Most in State." *Oshkosh Northwestern*, July 11.

Osinski, Alice. 1987. *The Chippewa*. Chicago: Childrens Press.

Ourada, Patricia K. 1990. *The Menominee*. New York: Chelsea House.

Oxley, Shelley. 1981. *The Anishinabe: An Overview Unit of the History and Background of the Wisconsin Ojibway Indian Tribe*. Madison, WI: American Indian Language and Culture Education Board.

———. 1981. *The History of the Menominee Indians.* Madison, WI: American Indian Language and Culture Education Board.

———. 1981. *The History of the Oneida Indians.* Madison, WI: American Indian Language and Culture Education Board.

———. 1981. *Keepers of the Fire: The History of the Potawatomi Indians of Wisconsin.* Madison, WI: American Indian Language and Culture Education Board.

Painter, Nell Irvin. 1994. "Representing Truth: Sojourner Truth's Knowing and Becoming Known." *The Journal of American History* 81 (September): 488–492.

Pang, Valerie O. and Robertta H. Barba. 1995. "The Power of Culture: Building Culturally Affirming Instruction." In *Educating for Diversity: An Anthology of Multicultural Voices,* edited by Carl A. Grant, 341–358. Boston: Allyn and Bacon.

Paul, Alec. 1999. "Our Stock of Food and Clothes." In *Native American Testimony: A Chronicle of Indian–White Relations From Prophecy to Present, 1492–2000,* rev. ed., edited by Peter Nabokov, 85–87. New York: Penguin.

Pellowski, Anne. 1982. *First Farm in the Valley: Anna's Story.* Winona, MN: Saint Mary's Press.

Peterson, Cris. 1994. *Extra Cheese, Please! Mozzarella's Journey from Cow to Pizza.* Honesdale, PA: Boyds Mills.

———. 1999. *Century Farm: 100 Years on a Family Farm.* Honesdale, PA: Boyds Mills.

Powers, Richard. 1977. "Wheat is King." *Badger History* 30 (March): 4–10.

Regguinti, Gordon. 1992. *The Sacred Harvest: Objibway Wild Rice Gathering.* Minneapolis, MN: Lerner.

Rendon, Marcie R. 1996. *Powwow Summer: A Family Celebrates the Circle of Life.* Minneapolis, MN: Carolrhoda Books.

Risinger, Frederick. 1992. "Trends in K–12 Social Studies." Eric Digest: ED351278: 1–5.

Rockwell, Anne. 2000. *Only Passing Through: The Story of Sojourner Truth.* New York: Alfred A. Knopf.

Rothstein-Fisch, Carrie, Patricia M. Greenfield, and Elise Trumball. 1999. "Bridging Cultures with Classroom Strategies." *Educational Leadership* 56 (April): 64–67.

Rudolph, Jack. 1982. "The Beaver Trade." *Cobblestone* 3 (June): 9–13.

Russell, George. 2000. *Native Americans FAQs Handbook*. Phoenix, AZ: Russell Publications.

Russell, Sharman. 1989. "The Early Years." *Cobblestone* 10 (February): 6–10.

Sahr, David E. 1997. "Native American Governments in Today's Curriculum." *Social Education* 61 (October): 308–315.

Sandmann, Alexa L. and John F. Ahern. 2002. *Linking Literature with Life: The NCSS Standards and Children's Literature for the Middle Grades*. Washington, DC: National Council for the Social Studies.

Santrey, Laurence. 1983. *Jim Thorpe Young Athlete*. Mahwah, NJ: Troll Associates.

Scheurmann, Geoffrey. 1998. "From Behaviorist to Constructivist Teaching." *Social Education* 62 (January): 6–9.

Schultz, Mary Ellen. 1985. *The Kelley Farm Activity Book*. St. Paul, MN: Minnesota Historical Society.

Scuro, Vincent. 1986. *Wonders of Dairy Cattle*. New York: Dodd, Mead.

Shemie, Bonnie. 1990. *Houses of Bark: Tipi, Wigwam, and Longhouse*. Montreal: Tundra Books.

Slapin, Beverly and Doris Seale, eds. 1998. *Through Indian Eyes: The Native Experience in Books for Children*. Berkeley, CA: Oyate.

Sleeter, Christine A. and Carl A. Grant. 1999. *Making Choices for Multicultural Education: Five Approaches to Race, Class, and Gender*, 3rd ed. Upper Saddle River, NJ: Merrill.

State Historical Society of Wisconsin. 1965. *The Days of the Lumberjack: Scenes From the Heyday of Lumbering*. Madison, WI: State Historical Society of Wisconsin.

Stockbridge-Munsee Historical Committee. 1993. *The History of the Stockbridge-Munsee Band of Mohican Indians*, 2nd ed. Bowler, WI: Muh-He-Con-Neew Press.

230

Stone, Lynn M. 1993. *Dairy Country*. Vero Beach, FL: Rourke.

Sullivan, George. 1994. *The Day the Women Got the Vote: A Photo History of the Women's Rights Movement*. New York: Scholastic.

Tanner, Helen Hornbeck. 1992. *The Ojibwa*. New York: Chelsea House.

Task Force on Scope and Sequence. 1989. "In Search of a Scope and Sequence for Social Studies." *Social Education* 53 (October): 376–385.

Taylor, Maureen. 1999. *Through the Eyes of Your Ancestors: A Step-by-Step Guide to Uncovering Your Family's History*. Boston: Houghton Mifflin Company.

Tomin, Barbara and Carol Burgoa. 1983. *Failure is Impossible: A Susan B. Anthony Biography*. Santa Rosa, CA: Tomin Burgoa Productions.

Van Hulst, Marguerite. 1971. "Dairy Cows." *Badger History* 24 (January):18–25.

Walker, Barbara M. 1979. *The Little House Cookbook: Frontier Foods From Laura Ingalls Wilder's Classic Stories*. New York: HarperTrophy.

Wilder, Laura Ingalls. 1971. *Little House in the Big Woods*. New York: HarperTrophy.

Wisconsin Paper Council. 1998. *Paper Makes Wisconsin Great*. Neenah, WI: Wisconsin Paper Council.

Wittstock, Laura Waterman. 1993. *Ininatig's Gift of Sugar: Traditional Native Sugarmaking*. Minneapolis, MN: Lerner.

Wolfman, Ira. 1991. *Do People Grow on Family Trees? Genealogy for Kids & Other Beginners*. New York: Workman Publishing.

Wooldridge, Connie Nordhielm. 2001. *When Esther Morris Headed West: Women, Wyoming, and the Right to Vote*. New York: Holiday House.

Zemelman, Steven, Harvey Daniels, and Arthur Hyde. 1998. *Best Practice: New Standards for Teaching and Learning in America's Schools*. Portsmouth, NH: Heinemann.

Ziegler, Sandra. 1987. *A Visit to the Dairy Farm*. Chicago: Childrens Press.